# Why Rousseau
# Was Wrong

# Why Rousseau Was Wrong

*Christianity and the Secular Soul*

*Frances Ward*

B L O O M S B U R Y
LONDON · NEW DELHI · NEW YORK · SYDNEY

First published in Great Britain 2013

A Continuum book

Bloomsbury Publishing Plc
50 Bedford Square
London WC1B 3DP

www.bloomsbury.com

Bloomsbury Publishing, London, New Delhi, New York and Sydney

Scripture quotations from The Authorized (King James) Version, the rights of which are vested in the Crown, are reproduced by permission of the Crown's patentee, Cambridge University Press.

A CIP record for this book is available from the British Library.

ISBN 978 1 4411 1553 9

10 9 8 7 6 5 4 3 2 1

Typeset by Fakenham Prepress Solutions, Fakenham, Norfolk NR21 8NN

Printed and bound by CPI Group (UK) Ltd, Croydon, CR0 4YY

*For Peter Powell*

# Author's Note

Alexander McCall Smith was kind enough to allow me to use passages from his Isabel Dalhousie series throughout the book, for which I am grateful.

# Contents

*Foreword* ix
*Introduction* 1

## Part One

1   The secular soul of Western culture  17

2   A brittle society  33

3   The legacy of liberal egalitarianism  49

## Part Two

4   Such a thing as society  69

5   From generation to generation  93

6   The Enlightenment story  111

## Part Three

7   The play of divine wisdom  125

8   The best that the Anglican Church can give  141

9   In whom we live and move and have our being  159

# Part Four

**10** Character produces hope 183

**11** Character building 195

**12** The role of education 215

*Conclusion* 235
*Postscript* 241
*Index of names* 243
*Index* 246

# Foreword

Most of us, I suspect, have experienced at one time or another in our lives a sense of being lost. It is a curious feeling. It is as if one has stepped out of a play in which one had a part and has become a spectator. That which had meaning and purpose has gone. It is a frame of mind in which one wonders, even if briefly, what is the point of continuing. It is, in a sense, a disintegration of the self, in which meaning eludes us. Fortunately for most of us such moments of doubt and despair are brief and we recover and continue with our day-to-day lives.

Societies as well as individuals can go wrong in this way. There are plenty of examples of social disintegration and perversity in which whole nations have been caught up in nihilistic or destructive patterns of thought and action. The twentieth century gave us Hitler, Stalin and Mao, along, of course, with less well-known instances of human evil in the shape of various local genocides and perversity. Human suffering and unhappiness has many faces.

Of course the idea that a modern liberal democracy can go seriously wrong will surprise many. How can a society such as Britain's be thought to be pursuing a fundamentally wrong path? How can such a society – well-fed and well-educated – be thought to be fundamentally flawed? Complacency lies behind such questioning, as was dramatically underlined by the widespread riots that recently inflamed London. The shocking violence and destructiveness of these events made people realise that perhaps all was not well in the society that they had thought so stable. For some the conclusion was a stark one: at the heart of this society lay an emptiness.

The diagnosis of the nature of this problem is a complex task. We know that there is something rotten, but what exactly is it? Following the London riots the search for an answer to this brought forth a whole raft of explanations, ranging from the simply material – those without material wealth will eventually do something to seize it – to more sophisticated analyses of social exclusion. Many of these explanations had credible features to them, but many failed to look closely enough at the prevailing orthodoxy of liberal individualism. Perhaps that is where the real fault lies. Perhaps we need one another rather more than liberal individualism is prepared to admit.

The subtle and convincing analysis in this profound and beautifully-written book throws a spotlight on this issue of our social failure. It reminds us, cogently and persuasively, that in spiritual activity conducted with others we are bound to one another in a way that strengthens both individuals and society as a whole. That is not a conclusion that will please those who deny the importance of the spiritual in our lives, but one might be tempted to ask them whether continued adherence to a brutal materialism is going to do anything to relieve the anxieties and distress of our contemporary condition. I am not convinced that continuing with our current materialist philosophy, with its individualistic focus, will do anything but increase our loneliness and unhappiness. Our spiritual garden in this country lies in ruins, and must be rebuilt if we are to thrive.

Frances Ward shows herself in this book to have a real understanding of what is wrong with contemporary Britain. We have created a desert in which the gods of materialism and greed have been worshipped at the expense of the values that gave life meaning. Her diagnosis is acute; the remedies suggested in this wise and compassionate book deserve very serious consideration. We need to listen.

Alexander McCall Smith

# Introduction

Rousseau wasn't wrong about everything, of course. He was the Father of the Romantic Movement which has given Western culture some of its finest poetry, literature, music and art. But he was also the Father of a number of other key Enlightenment ideas that have proved popular and pervasive, which have shaped the secular soul and, arguably, left Western culture rather brittle as a result. Nor was he alone; other Enlightenment thinkers besides him thought they were at the beginning of a new era, where anything was possible, and the soul of humanity could be moulded to fit new ideas, leaving behind the traditions of the Dark Ages, moving onwards into the light of a dawning age. Such ideas had the exhilaration of utopian dreams. They were innovative and looked to the future, believing in human progress, instead of the dead, tired, often corrupt traditions of the past. Many of those ideas have left a tremendous legacy. But some have not.

I've used the term 'the soul' as short-hand for the values and attitudes that represent someone's often unexamined view on life. Such values and attitudes, in Western culture today, do not tend to be informed by Christianity any more but by what can be loosely called 'secular humanism'. Secular humanism is a difficult phenomenon to define with any success, and probably best seen as a large umbrella, sheltering a great many different and nuanced ideas that inform values, attitude and therefore behaviour. Given that, I try to answer the question: what are the philosophical ideas that have shaped the secular soul? That question has taken me back to the Enlightenment, and particularly, although not exclusively, to Jean-Jacques Rousseau.

I suggest that how 'the soul' is formed has a fundamental impact upon what the human person looks like. The human person today (as ever) is a complex creature, suggesting that the soul that shapes that person is complex also. Often what emerges in any particular time is a reaction to what went before and, if Christianity does not form the soul of many today, that is largely because Christianity is taken to be a negative influence, oppressive in the values it prescribes, and making truth claims (about the existence of God, for example) which do not stand up to the rationalism of today's scientific world view. The secular humanism that shapes the soul instead will tend towards atheism (the belief that there is no God, in the traditional Christian sense of the word). It will tend towards a set of ethical values based on the Golden Rule ('do unto others as you would have them do to you'). The secular humanist will usually assume that humanity is basically good and means well, with compassion and tolerance held as key values. Its politics will often be informed by a liberal egalitarianism that foregrounds equality and fairness, choice, freedom and autonomy. It rates happiness as a goal in life. The secular soul thinks highly of itself, on the whole, and often for good reason, for there are many commendable, benign qualities that it holds dear.

On the other hand, the secular soul has some dark shadows. Because it was born of the Enlightenment, it tends to believe in itself and its own capacity to solve problems and change things for the good. Consequently, it can be loath to examine those shadows (unlike the Christian soul, which, it is often claimed, can be overly keen to confess its sins and guilt-trip others).

So let us imagine the secular soul up there, on the stage, in the limelight, with three spotlights trained on it. Enlightened, believing in itself, this soul is not used to looking behind. But three shadows fall away, stretching towards the closing darkness. It is an audition. What might this secular soul say of itself? We might first hear it saying, plausibly, that it thinks of itself as an autonomous individual, keen to stand out from the crowd. And second, perhaps, it understands itself to be purposeful, and useful. It has direction, and focus, it is forward-looking and strategic. And, third, it knows itself to have an identity. It gives the markers, sends out the signals, describing its identity with this label or that.

Three seemingly attractive and good qualities but which, I suggest, cast three shadows. The first shadow is excessive individualism. The second, a utilitarian and instrumental mindset that forgets the difference between purpose and meaning. The third shadow, a preoccupation with 'identity', now a possession, worn like a badge. I argue that we are haunted by these three shadows, which diminish the human person, making a darkness at the heart of the secular soul. To the detriment of Western culture.

This book is about the failure of some key Enlightenment ideas as they shape the soul, the human person and, consequently, Western culture. I suggest that a culture is only as good as its soul and that Western societies discard the traditions of Christianity at their peril. For Christianity is very aware, traditionally, of the shadows of humanity (you need only to read Thomas à Kempis' *The Imitation of Christ*[1] to discover that). Christianity, from its earliest days, has shaped the soul to be corporate rather than individualistic. The Christian soul has been encouraged to find meaning in time, in nature, in practices, in things and people, so such things are not merely means to some end or useful, but point to an end beyond themselves, which Christians call God. And rather than seeing the

---

[1] Thomas à Kempis, *The Imitation of Christ*, Harold C. Gardner, S.J., (ed.), Doubleday, 1955.

human person as having an identity, the Christian faith provides formative practices that enable a virtuous character to develop.

The human personality looks very different with a Christian soul. Arguably, society functions better too.

# Interlude

Isabel Dalhousie is the fictional creation of Alexander McCall Smith, also known for the Number One Lady Detective. Like Precious Ramotswe, Isabel dabbles in detecting (in Edinburgh rather than Botswana), but her real interest is moral philosophy. Isabel is forever wondering about the state we're in, and what it means to live a good life today. Every so often, in what follows, Isabel has something to say, and I've thought it best simply to let her interrupt.

> Sub specie aeternitatis, *she thought: In the context of eternity, this is nothing, as are all our human affairs. In the context of eternity, our anxieties, our doubts, are little things, of no significance. Or, as Herrick put it, rose buds were there to be gathered, because really, she thought, there was no proof of life beyond this one; and all that mattered, therefore, was that happiness and love should have their chance, their brief chance, in this life, before annihilation and the nothingness to which we were all undoubtedly heading, even our sun, which was itself destined for collapse and extinction, signifying the end of the party for whomsoever was left.*
>
> *But she knew, even as she thought this, that we cannot lead our lives as if nothing really mattered. Our concerns might be small things, but they loomed large to us. The crushing underfoot of an ants' nest was nothing to us, but to the ants it was a cataclysmic disaster: the ruination of a city, the laying waste of a continent. There were worlds within worlds, and each will have within its confines values and meaning. It may not really matter to the world*

*at large, thought Isabel, that I should feel happy rather than sad, but*
*it matters to me, and the fact that it matters matters.*[2]

So we develop the three themes a little further.

# Individual or corporate?

Excessive individualism was identified as the most significant social
evil by the Joseph Rowntree Foundation report of 2009.[3] It is a basic
assumption of today's world: that we are individuals. It goes like this:
'I am an individual. Along with other individuals, I make up society.
Because I have contracted into society, I have rights to things, to be
treated in a certain way'. It's such a basic view that it has become
second nature. But it has not always been like this.

In fact the word 'individual' means 'indivisible' or 'not able to be
divided from the whole'. That is certainly how John Donne understood
the word at the beginning of the seventeenth century in his oft-quoted
passage 'No man is an island'. A major premise of this book is that instead
of a first-person singular mentality, we need to begin with a first-person
plural understanding.[4] The corporate before the individual. 'We' before 'I'.

To say 'we' does not, though, mean that the individual is oblit-
erated. It is a real fear, and an understandable one, given the (atheist)
ideologies of the twentieth century, where communism and fascism
subsumed the individual under terrifying collectives.[5] The memory
of the twentieth century is still vivid, and you can see why, in Western

---

[2] Alexander McCall Smith, *The Right Attitude to Rain*, Little, Brown, London, 2006, p. 214.

[3] David Utting (ed.), *Contemporary Social Evils*, Joseph Rowntree Foundation, Policy Press, Bristol, Portland, 2009.

[4] See Roger Scruton on 'corporate personality' in *Gentle Regrets: Thoughts From a Life*, Continuum, London and New York, 2005, p. 80.

[5] Peter Hitchens is good on this. See Chapter 6 'Homo sovieticus' and Chapter 9 'Are conflicts fought in the name of religion conflicts about religion?' in his *The Rage Against God*, Continuum, London and New York, 2010.

societies, we might want to ensure that the individual has autonomy and freedom.

Nevertheless, I maintain that humanity is primarily corporate. Christianity is particularly good at being corporate, and has been since St Paul first wrote about what it might mean in his letters to the Christians in Corinth (an ancient city, which was incredibly diverse in the first century AD), in Galatia, Philippi, Thessalonia and Rome among other places. His words have had a profound influence through the ages on the development of political theory. It is an interesting history, as we explore further below.

## Purpose or meaning?

Charles Taylor's book *A Secular Age* tells the story of a utilitarian or instrumental rationality that has become a defining feature of the modern era.[6] You can see it whenever, for example, education is reduced to measured outcomes, league tables, or is talked about as a means to a good career or to the acquisition of skills. As a society we have become very purpose-driven and very good at valuing things in terms of their usefulness. A utilitarian society produces a diminished sense of what it means to be a human being. Instead we need to recapture what it is to be and do things for their own sake.

A good illustration is friendship. You do not keep friends very long if you only make them because of what they can do for you. A utilitarian approach to friendship quickly fails. Friendship is an end in itself. It is not utilitarian (useful) or instrumental (a means to an end). It is for its own sake, although it will also be of mutual benefit in many ways. Play is another example. A child at play does

---

[6] Charles Taylor, *A Secular Age*, Belkap Press of Harvard University Press, Cambridge, MA. and London, 2007.

it for its own sake, although there will be important learning, as Winnicott pointed out, as the child learns to negotiate with reality.[7] The quality of the play will vary enormously, reflecting how alive and open we are to different possibilities, and the work of the imagination. There is no utility to this; the outcome is purely for its own sake, often an exploration of meaning. The wisdom gained cannot be measured. I suggest that as a society we find it increasingly difficult to do and be in this playful way, at any real depth. We tend to see ourselves, and others, as a means to some useful end, serving some purpose.

This is what makes education so important, in any society, and society reflects the sort of education its children receive. Education has to be meaningful rather than purposeful. It needs to be for its own sake.[8] When it is for its own sake, then education becomes personally and culturally enriching and society is richer too. Education like this is also the best way of providing young (and old) people with the wherewithal to counter the cultural impoverishment that afflicts a materialistic society.

*She was surprised: she had not expected Grace to know the meaning of the Latin phrase, but she immediately realised that her assumption*

---

[7] D.W. Winnicott, *Playing and Reality*, Routledge, London, 1971.

[8] Phillip Blond makes the point that education should be free of political control, for 'If the true political goal is one of virtuous flourishing and a continuous debate as to the nature of the good life, politics itself is part of the educative process and in consequence should not wish to subordinate the process of education to itself'. He bemoans the fact that the education syllabus 'is increasingly conceived in utilitarian, functionalist terms, such that children are only to learn what will benefit the state, including the state by way of the market'. *Red Tory: How Left and Right have Broken Britain and How We Can Fix It*, Faber and Faber, London, 2010, p. 174. Chris Woodhead says something similar when he writes '... the Government's utilitarian obsessions have, in my view, undermined belief in the intrinsic value of academic study, and will, if this philistinism continues, threaten the character of universities, like Oxford and Cambridge, that still have a global reputation for academic excellence' in *A Desolation of Learning: Is this the Education our Children Deserve?* Pencil-Sharp Publications, Petersfield, 2009, p. 3.

*was condescending. It was as if she had said to herself: housekeepers don't know Latin. And in general, they did not, but it was wrong to imagine that somebody who happens to have such a job in life should not know such things. And that, surely, was what education was all about: it should make it possible for everybody to have the consolations of literature – and Latin, too – to accompany them in their work, whatever it turned out to be. The bus driver who knows his Robert Burns, the waitress who reads Jane Austen or who goes on her day off to look at an exhibition of Vermeers: these are the quiet triumphs of education, Isabel thought. It's why education was justified for its own sake, and not as a means to some vocational end.*[9]

## Me and my identity!

My third theme is related to excessive individualism, for what do individuals have? They have 'identities'. 'Me and my identity'. To hear someone talk about identity, it can sound like a possession. My 'identity' – or 'identities' – for very quickly they proliferate. And our 'identities' can start to conflict too, which does not make life easy.

'Identity speak' is thin, and wears out if you examine it too closely. Although you can see its attractions.

*They were both silent for a moment. Their conversations had started in the deep end, unlike most conversations, which launched themselves into the shallowest of shallows.*

*Isabel had not finished. 'Identity's difficult. I suppose it brings about social cohesion, but it's not much fun if you don't quite fit. Being gay, for example, used to be pretty miserable. Or being a Protestant in a place like Ireland when the Catholic Church ruled*

---

[9] Alexander McCall Smith, *The Forgotten Affairs of Youth*, Little, Brown, London, 2011, p. 135.

*the roost. Or being a woman in Ireland under the thumb of all those priests. Those big, dominant identities have been weakened, I suppose, but that might be a good thing, on balance. It's allowed other identities to flourish.'*

*Jane did not look convinced. 'Yes, but if you weaken identity, people end up not knowing who they are. They end up living bland lives with no real content to them. No customs, no traditions, no sense of their past. And I think one needs to know who one is.' She hesitated. 'I guess we've spent so much time feeling ashamed of ourselves, it's made us rather apologetic about being what we are. As a result we don't want to be anything.'*

*Isabel was intrigued. 'Ashamed of our history?'*

*'Yes. After all, we forced ourselves on others. We despoiled and plundered the world. Destroyed cultures left, right and centre.'*

*'Perhaps.'*

*'But we did! No perhaps about it. We did!'*

*'Well, at least Australia's said sorry,' observed Isabel. 'I'm not so sure that the West as a whole has. And even if we did all those things, we also invented penicillin and computers and human rights. We don't need to be ashamed of any of that.'*

*Jane sighed. 'No, we can't browbeat ourselves for too long.'*[10]

Identity can be something to hold onto in a troubled world; an easy way of labelling yourself, or others, to signify a sense of belonging. But like any label, when you start to unpick it, it doesn't reveal much underneath. There is a better way of thinking about the human person.

*She had changed ... she had become more forgiving, more under-standing of human weaknesses than she had been in her twenties.*

---

[10] McCall Smith, *The Forgotten Affairs of Youth*, pp. 34–5.

*And love, too, had become more important to her; not love in the*
*erotic sense, which obeyed its own tides throughout life and could be*
*as intense, as unreasonable in its demands, whatever age one was,*
*but love in the sense of agape, the brotherly love of others, which was*
*a subtle presence that became stronger as the years passed; that, at*
*least, was what had happened with her.*

*'So there's not much that we can do about that central bit of*
*ourselves – the core?' she had asked. Would you call it that – the core?'*

*'A good enough name for it,' said Richard. 'No, I don't think there's*
*much we can do about that. The very deep bits of us, the real prefer-*
*ences, are there whether we like it or not. But if these deep bits are*
*not very pleasant we can keep them under control. We can adapt*
*them.' ... 'And I suppose we can develop positive attitudes which*
*mean that in our dealings with others, in our day-to-day lives, we*
*behave a bit better.'*[11]

Character is something that can change and develop, depending
on what habits we adopt and how we cultivate some traits, and not
others. This understanding of what it means to be a human person is
one we will return to. It has much to commend it.

## A little like playing in an orchestra

When someone plays in an orchestra, the corporate, the meaning
and the character are crucial. The performer is distinctive because of
the instrument she plays, and because of the individuality she brings
to the whole. A bassoonist, or a cellist; a flautist or a timpanist, she
will contribute as an individual, playing a distinctive instrument and
her individuality is essential. But the whole is primary; the orchestra
has a corporate personality and it is greater than the sum of its parts.

---

[11] McCall Smith, *The Right Attitude to Rain*, p. 30.

The member of an orchestra may at times have to defend music against those Gradgrindians who say that it has no purpose. 'What is the use of beauty?', 'Why bother?' they cry. 'What's the point in the arts? In doing all that practice, honing skills and talents over years?' Such utilitarian arguments need to be countered by saying that life has meaning and it's worth exploring, through the arts, and through religion.

Although the performer has a particular personality that contributes ('I am a violinist'), her individual identity must not dominate. She must have the depth of character to be able to merge into the background, or assume the foreground, in obedience to the interpretation and direction of the conductor. In short, she needs to be corporate, believe in meaning and have character.

## Gang culture

It becomes rather important to think about ourselves in this way because 'identity' can actually close down individuality. The temptation is strong to join with others who share the same identity and form a collective. Gang culture begins here when there is pressure to join with the strongest 'identity' around. David Lammy MP describes the male youth culture of Tottenham like this.

> Theirs is the world of the alpha male, where 'respect' is everything. Look at someone the wrong way, or stray into the wrong postcode, and you could lose your life. Carry a knife or a gun and you are a real man. Become a 'babyfather', have children with a string of different women, and people will look up to you. No one ever taught these boys that the inability to delay gratification, the obsession with status symbols and a worldview centred on the self are markers not of manhood, but of immaturity.[12]

---

[12] David Lammy, *Out of the Ashes: Britain after the Riots*, Guardian Books, London, 2011, p.97.

'Collective' grouping like this, which is a tribal mentality, is very different to how I am presenting the 'corporate'. A gang is a very different animal to an orchestra. The corporate, as St Paul explained, incorporates different members and sustains their distinctions. As I use the word, the collective demands the suppression of real individuality. You have to become the same as all the rest to belong. And so a collective will often be age-specific (you won't find people of other ages joining in), or culture-specific (you need to speak and dress the same), or post-code specific (woe betide you if you stray).

The corporate, on the other hand, will include difference. A team requires each person to bring different skills. An orchestra incorporates different players, different personalities and thrives on the distinctive gifts that each member brings. So should churches, where worshippers are constantly reminded of what it means to be corporate, rather than collective. It is a constant all-too-human temptation to become collective rather than corporate, to stick with people who are like you, and not to embrace those who are different. Churches sometimes succumb to that temptation and become collectives. But they should not and, as we shall see, the central action of the Church, the sacrament of Holy Communion, is a reminder – even a mandate – to be corporate.

Ultimately, your 'identity' doesn't matter that much. If doesn't matter if you are gay, what gender you are, or if you are transgendered; whether you see yourself as a member of a minority of any kind. It does not even, ultimately, matter if you are rich or poor (although Jesus did say it was easier for a camel to pass through the eye of a needle than for the rich to enter the Kingdom of God)[13]. Of course, though, when groups suffer oppression, solidarity is essential. But that solidarity can become counter-productive, if it is sustained

---

[13]  Matthew, Chapter 19, Verse 24.

when the oppression is lifted, as Hannah Arendt observed.[14] What matters is the sort of character you have: how trustworthy you are; that you are not greedy or cruel; and that you know how to be kind to others. It matters to be able to be generous with what you have, even if it hurts your own self-interest; that you know how to put others first, and not insist on your own agenda.

It matters to have character and not just an identity. With character, you know you need to develop emotionally and morally, and you know that virtue is important. And, contrary to how much we hear about happiness, if you strive to be virtuous you quickly realise that happiness is only ever yours when you have been kind or good. Happiness is always a by-product of virtue, never an end in itself. If you seek happiness for its own sake, it will always elude you.[15]

These three themes focus on different ways to be human. Western society today is excessively individualistic, as many recognise. I think we would fare better if we concentrated on being corporate, in the sense that St Paul and John Donne meant. We tend towards a utilitarian mindset that turns people and things into means to our ends,

---

[14] In Hannah Arendt, Chapter 1 'On Humanity in Dark Times: Thoughts about Lessing' in *Men in Dark Times*, Harcourt Brace, San Diego, CA., New York and London, 1968. Hannah Arendt noticed that when faced with the oppression of the Holocaust, Jews gathered together in solidarity. Under the pressure of persecution, the Jewish people in the ghettoes move so closely together that the distances between them collapsed. A warmth of human relationship resulted, which 'can breed a kindliness and sheer goodness of which human beings are otherwise scarcely capable' (p. 13). It also created a sense of 'being unburdened by care for the world' (p. 14). Arendt argued that after the oppression was lifted, if the sense of solidarity persisted, it could be misleading and dangerous, because it did not reach beyond itself, had no sense of responsibility for society as a whole, and did not create humanity and develop the polis.

[15] There is a large and growing literature on 'happiness'. Richard Layard's work is worth reading, *Happiness: Lessons from a New Science*, Allen Lane, London and New York, 2005, and so is Christopher Jamison, *Finding Happiness: Monastic Steps for a Fulfilling Life*, Phoenix, London, 2008, who writes with the connection between happiness and virtue in mind.

and stresses the useful and purposeful. By enhancing the cultural enrichment that education can offer, human beings become ends in themselves, imaginative, with moral resource and emotional intelligence, seeking meaning in life. We get hung up on our 'identities' and defensive if they are under attack. When we see ourselves as having an 'identity' we can quickly assume a herd mentality. How much better, I suggest, it is to focus on what makes for a good character, where we strive to be virtuous, to be kind, gentle, patient and trustworthy. We should also be rather more critical of 'happiness' as the best goal in life, and see happiness, rather, as a by-product of virtuous behaviour.

So – a taster of what is to come. Shortly we will journey back to summer 2011, and take note of the riots that fired off in many major cities of Britain. Although 2012 saw major reasons to celebrate as a nation with the Diamond Jubilee and then the Olympics in London, I think it remains the case that Britain is a brittle place to live, largely because the secular soul has such an influence on our current mindset. But many of the challenges that face Britain face other Western cultures too, and as I examine the social and economic neo-liberalism of Thatcher and the Blair/Brown years we will be looking at trends that have become dominant since the 1960s and 1970s within Western societies more generally. Each of our themes can be identified within a social and political revolution, provoking a series of fundamental changes that have happened since the 1970s. I argue that those changes find their roots in the Enlightenment, and are basically contrary to a Christian world view.

Throughout we are going to pursue each of our three themes in different ways, digging into the subsoil of our social imaginary to discover what has fed our contemporary mindset and shaped the secular soul. This will include a turn to novels and contemporary writing for a different wisdom, to feed the imagination in other ways. I offer some thoughts about how Western culture might become less brittle through education and a revitalising of civil society.

# *Part One*

# 1

# *The secular soul of Western culture*

Living in Britain today is tough. There's a great deal we can be thankful for, in comparison to some parts of the world. But, as I write in late 2012, with a successful Olympics behind us, we are still in a recession that is biting deeply, and there is widespread discontent with the way things are politically and economically.[1]

The winter of 2011 saw occupy camps in a number of major British cities, most notably at St Paul's Cathedral in London. People were protesting at the state we're in. Many faced unemployment and the impact of government cuts – cuts in benefits, in pensions, both in the private and the public sector – because the national debt was serious. The rhetoric was of 'austerity', but the word had a nostalgic ring that

---

[1] Phillip Blond puts it like this: 'We all know the symptoms: increasing fear, lack of trust and abundance of suspicion, long-term increase in violent crime, loneliness, recession, depression, private and public debt, family break-up, divorce, infidelity, bureaucratic and unresponsive public services, dirty hospitals, powerlessness, the rise of racism, excessive paperwork, longer and longer working hours, children who have no parents, concentrated and seemingly irremovable poverty, the permanence of inequality, teenagers with knives, teenagers being knifed, the decline of politeness, aggressive youths, the erosion of our civil liberties and the increase of obsessive surveillance, public authoritarianism, private libertarianism, general pointlessness, political cynicism and a pervading lack of daily joy', *Op. cit.* p. 1.

did not seem to do justice to the anxieties people faced of personal debt and the terrible poverty that always seems to hit the poorest, in cities that struggle the most.

In part the anger was fuelled by media and press reports of a culture in the finance sector where bank and company CEOs earn basic salaries that sound exorbitant, augmented by bonuses and free shares and hefty pension contributions. The disparity between the rich and the poor seemed ever widening to the general public. Social, or responsible, capitalism, the rhetoric of the coalition government of the day, was unlikely to succeed without a greater sense of cohesion in society. For it to be credible, 'responsible capitalism' required a renewed sense of moral responsibility in society and a re-assessment of the notions of public service and the common good, instead of the general sense of distrust and lack of expectation of honesty prevalent in the early months of 2012.

But it was not only the rich who emerged as self-interested. The riots of the summer of 2011 revealed a face of Britain that was profoundly ugly, with thousands of people turning out, motivated by greed and resentment. The extensive rioting in the major cities of Britain left many with a sense of ill ease. Some analysis has been done,[2] and we shall examine it in the light of the legacy of the neo-liberalism of Thatcher, and a decade and a half of New Labour. As I write, the coalition government of Conservative and Liberal Democrats is seeking to offer something different, a more consensual style, but struggles to be convincing. There is not only a sense of 'burn out', yes, of the old 'Left' and 'Right', but also of the neo-liberal trajectory of Thatcher, and the New Labour Blair/Brown years. The new rhetoric of 'Big Society' has

---

[2] See Dan Roberts (ed.) *Reading the Riots*, Guardian Books, 2011, Kindle Version 1.0, available at http://www.amazon.co.uk/Reading-Riots-Investigating-Englands-ebook/dp/B006LL)CII and Lammy, *op. cit.*

left most unconvinced that it provides a sufficient vision to capture the imagination of the nation and, as the government fails to follow up the rhetoric, with positive incentives to support philanthropy and help organisations with the responsibility to strengthen civic life.

In such an uncertain climate, it is instructive to go more deeply and examine some of the philosophical foundations that shape contemporary Western culture and its mindset. I have called it the secular soul, as a shorthand to describe what might be referred to, variously, as the public mind, ideology, social imaginary and national psyche.[3] The assumptions we make as a Western culture about what it means to be a human person in today's world need some analysis, for our 'anthropology' (how we understand the human being) ultimately gives us our society. The secular soul begins at the Enlightenment, I argue, and it is an interesting history to uncover its roots. There are other traditions and practices, though: alternative historical, philosophical and theological resources that shape the soul differently. These traditions extend back through the Middle Ages, to the early Church and the writings of St Paul.

The reader is commended to think afresh about what Christianity, and particularly church worship with its significant continuities of practice through the centuries, has to offer when viewed as a resource

---

[3] 'Social imaginary' is the expression used by Charles Taylor in his *A Secular Age*. He says it's the default background 'taken-for-granted' assumptions that most people make. He writes: 'I speak of "imaginary" (i) because I'm talking about the way ordinary people "imagine" their social surroundings ... But it is also the case that (ii) theory is often the possession of a small minority, whereas what is interesting in the social imaginary is that it is shared by large groups of people, if not the whole society. Which leads to a third difference: (iii) the social imaginary is that common understanding which makes possible common practices, and a widely shared sense of legitimacy.' Taylor says that any current social imaginary becomes so embedded that it seems the only possible one, the only one which makes sense: 'It begins to define the contours of the world, and can eventually come to count as the taken-for-granted shape of things, too obvious to mention.' *A Secular Age*, The Belkap Press of Harvard University Press, Cambridge, MA and London, 2007, pp. 171ff.

for understanding our three themes. Every so often the reader will be
required to think theologically about some of these issues. 'Theology'
is not always a discipline that receives much approbation, to say the
least. Often it is used as a term of dismissal in social and political
circles. 'That's just theology!' you will hear people say. But proper
theological thinking can offer insights that we cannot find elsewhere.
I ask you to come with an open mind if theology is not your usual
reading, with an imagination prepared to be stretched out of its
normal compass.

## What if we really did kill God, what then?

*Would it really be as William Golding had predicted in* Lord of
the Flies? *The thesis behind that was that children left to their own
devices reverted to savagery, but it was really just a mirror image of
the savagery of the adult world; remove the adults and the children
fell into tribalism and superstition. But if the resulting childish
dystopia merely reflected the adult world, then what happened if
one removed the adults – in other words, the authority figures –
from the adult world? What if we really did kill God, what then?
Would we all be rationally committed to the greater good, or would
savagery be the norm? To kill God: the idea was absurd. If God
existed, then he should be above being killed, by definition. But if he
was just something in which we believed, or hoped, perhaps, killing
him may be an act of cruelty that would rebound on us; like telling
small children that fairies were impossible, that Jack never had a
beanstalk; or telling a teenager that love was an illusion, a chemical
response to a chemical situation. There were things, she thought,
which were probably true, but which we simply should not always
acknowledge as true; novels, for example – always false, elaborately
constructed deceptions, but we believed them to be true while we*

*were reading them; we had to, as otherwise there was no point. One would read, and all the time as one read, one would say, mentally, He didn't really.*[4]

Isabel is agnostic about whether God exists. Mostly, it seems, she does not believe. But at other times we find her hoping that there is more to life than meets the eye. Often when we eavesdrop on her internal dialogue, or in conversation with her friends, we find her wondering about philosophical and moral issues. Here she is now, for example, wondering if Nietzsche was right, whether we've killed God. What if we really did kill God, what then?

Without God, she wonders, would society revert to savagery? The spectre of Hobbes (1588–1679) haunts her words. Hobbes wrote in the seventeenth century; indeed, his life spanned some of most crucial changes that laid down political life as we know it in Britain today.[5] Hobbes presented us with a thought experiment. 'How did society begin?' he asked. He suggested that individuals, tired of living lives that were solitary, poor, nasty, brutish and short, came together to establish a contract. That contract created society for the mutual benefit of its members. The idea of the social contract caught on, and influenced his contemporaries and those who followed, particularly John Locke (1632–1704), and Jean-Jacques Rousseau (1712–78). Each thought that the basic building block for society was the individual. Society followed when individuals contracted together and political life began.

---

[4] Alexander McCall Smith, *The Comfort of Saturdays*, Little, Brown, London, 2008, p. 41.
[5] Hobbes' birth was brought on, it's said, by the fear of the imminent arrival of the Armada during the reign of Elizabeth I. In his time, James VI of Scotland became James I, with the Act of Union; Charles I was executed in 1649 for claiming too much 'Divine Right' to rule; he lived through the Civil War, and then the 11-year Protectorate of Oliver Cromwell; saw the restoration of the Stuart Dynasty with Charles II, but died before the Glorious Revolution of 1688, when James II was forced into exile, and the Protestant William and Mary acceded to the British throne.

What also followed, from the Enlightenment onwards, was a sense that society could be re-created and renewed. That it is possible to start again, and again, to build the perfect society. The old traditions of the Church and mediaeval society were thrown out: innovation became the way to do things. Revolution and ideological blueprints. New this, new that, and so modernity arrived. Utopian futures in human hands.

Such thinking is embedded in our psyche in the West today. Social contract theory we take for granted, and the sense that we can make things better by starting anew. I argue here, though, that the political thought-experiments of the Enlightenment have left us not particularly enlightened at all.[6] That, in fact, it would be better if we looked back before Hobbes and the other *Philosophes*, to a different set of ideas. Ideas that do not assume that the individual is the basic building block of society, but rather that we start (and end) our lives as social beings, within society that is something much more enduring that the individual. Society understood this way carries its wisdom through time by traditions and institutional life. I would like to suggest that such traditions are more helpful to us than a belief in

---

[6] I'm not the only one who thinks this. David Bentley Hart is deliciously scathing about what he calls 'the ideology of the "modern" and the myth of "the Enlightenment": '... what many of us are still in the habit of calling the "Age of Reason" was in many significant ways the beginning of the eclipse of reason's authority as a cultural value; that the modern age is notable in large measure for the triumph of inflexible and unthinking dogmatism in every sphere of human endeavour (including the sciences) and for a flight from rationality to any number of soothing fundamentalisms, religious and secular; that the Enlightenment ideology of modernity *as such* does not even deserve any particular credit for the advance of modern science; that the modern secular state's capacity for barbarism exceeds any of the evils for which Christendom might justly be indicted, not solely by virtue of the superior technology at its disposal, but by its very nature; that among the chief accomplishments of modern culture have been a massive retreat to superstition and the gestation of especially pitiless forms of nihilism; and that, by comparison to the Christian revolution it succeeded, modernity is little more than an aftereffect, or even counterrevolution – a reactionary flight back to a comfortable, but dehumanizing, mental and moral servitude to elemental nature.' *Atheist Delusions: The Christian Revolution and Its Fashionable Enemies*, Yale University Press, New Haven, CT. and London, 2009, pp. xi–xii.

innovation and 'change for change's sake' with its utopian attempt to realise some dream or blueprint of a better state of affairs.

Isabel Dalhousie sidestepped the question of the *existence* of God, or at least, refused to tackle it in a ding-dong way. She was wise.[7]

## Friends in mind

I have a number of close friends who do not share my Christian faith. It is an interesting phenomenon, friendship with those with whom you differ fundamentally about something important. It can feel like the sensation in a missing limb.[8] It depends on the friend, of course, but it is as if some absence haunts your intimacy. Some things I just do not say. Perhaps because I am anxious not to come over as 'religious' and so confirm the stereotype. Much common ground there may be, but, however much the friendship means – and my friends mean a great deal to me – something is missing that cannot be shared. A beautiful natural scene, or piece of religious music, and I want to sing of the gift of God in creation or in human endeavour. But do not.

Isabel is talking with her friend Jamie, a bassoonist.

> *'Mozart, you see,' he said, 'is so perfect. If there can be music like that, it must be tied in some way to something outside us – it has to be. Some combination of harmony and shape that has nothing to*

---

[7] Although, if you want a good theological introduction to the debates with the New Atheists, as they are called, I'd recommend David Bentley Hart (just cited): 'But atheism that consists entirely in vacuous arguments afloat on oceans of historical ignorance, made turbulent by storms of strident self-righteousness, is as contemptible as any other form of dreary fundamentalism' p. 4; also Roger Scruton, *The Face of God, The Gifford Lectures 2010*, Continuum, London and New York, 2012. Also, Jonathan Sacks, *The Great Partnership: God, Science and the Search for Meaning*, Hodder, London 2011.

[8] With thanks to Stephen Prickett for this metaphor. See his *Modernity and the Reinvention of Tradition: Backing into the Future*, Cambridge University Press, Cambridge, New York, Melbourne, 2009, p. 219. The book is very good on the history of 'tradition.'

*do with us – it's just there. Maybe God's something to do with that.
Something to do with beauty.'*

Something to do with beauty. *Yes, she thought, that was one way
of expressing it. Moral beauty existed as clearly as any other form of
beauty and perhaps that was where we would find the God who was
so vividly, and sometimes bizarrely, described in our noisy religious
explanations. It was an intriguing thought, as it meant that a concert
could be a spiritual experience, a secular painting a religious icon, a
beguiling face a passing angel.*[9]

# 'I just can't believe in God'

'I just can't believe in God', say my secular humanist friends. I say
to them, put aside, for a moment, the question of the existence of
God. It's a good question, but it is not the only one. Think instead
about what sort of society you want to live in, and what makes that
society resilient. Suspend, for a while – at least for the duration of this
book – that Cartesian, or Humean, rationalism that takes nothing
on trust – no institutions, no traditional knowledge – but insists on
subjecting all givens to the radical test of doubt, with experience the
only criterion for knowledge.[10] That sort of rationality is prevalent
in our society. It is a key aspect of our modern condition, that
critical approach. But, for the moment, go with me, and consider
the proposition that Descartes does not have the monopoly on ways

---

[9] Alexander McCall Smith, *The Lost Art of Gratitude*, Little, Brown, London, 2009, p. 190,
emphasis original.

[10] The test of Dawkins, Harris, Dennett, Hitchens. Scruton makes the comment: 'The
violence of the diatribes uttered by these evangelical atheists is indeed remarkable. After
all, the Enlightenment happened three centuries ago; the arguments of Hume, Kant and
Voltaire have been absorbed by every educated person. What more is there to be said? And
if you must say it, why say it so stridently?' "The Return of Religion" in Mark Dooley (ed.),
*The Roger Scruton Reader*, Continuum, London and New York, 2009, p. 128.

of knowing. In what follows, I ask you to hold that radical doubt in radical doubt. Perhaps there are other ways of knowing things.

*'I can't believe in God, Miss Dalhousie. I've tried from time to time and I just can't. And yet, when we need them, who are the people who are always there for us? Who are the people who comfort us? Whom would you like to have at your ending? What kind of person would you like to have at your death bed? An atheist or somebody with faith?'*

*Isabel thought. Were there not atheists who were just as capable of giving love and support as others? And might it not be better to die in doubt, if that had been one's condition in life?*

*'I know some very sympathetic non-believers,' she said. 'I don't think we should discount them.'*

*'Maybe,' said Florence. 'But there's nothing in the atheist's creed that says he must love others, is there?'*

*Isabel could not let this pass. 'But he may have every reason! Even if you do not believe in God you may still think it very important to act towards others with generosity and consideration. That's what morality is all about.'*

*Florence's eyes lit up. 'Yes,' she said, 'morality – the ordinary variety – says that you shouldn't do anything to hurt others. But I'm not so sure that it tells you to go further, to love them.' She thought for a moment. 'And surely most people are not going to make the effort to love others on the basis of some theory, are they? I know that I wouldn't. We have to learn these things. We have to have them drummed into us.'*

*'The moral habits of the heart,' mused Isabel.*

*'Yes,' said Florence. 'And religion is rather good at doing that, don't you think?'*[11]

---

[11] McCall Smith, *The Right Attitude to Rain*, p. 94.

# Does religion poison everything?

After the strident atheism of Ditchkins, as Terry Eagleton has
coined them (Dawkins and Hitchins),[12] the assertion that religion
poisons everything[13] is under review with Alain de Botton's latest
book *Religion for Atheists*. He considers an alternative possibility
that religion has bestowed many benefits upon human civilisation.
He thinks atheists should take the best of those benefits, and build
temples of rationalism that emulate the awe and wonder of religious
buildings. Religion is 'a good thing', now, it seems, but we can leave
God out of the picture.[14]

At least de Botton has the honesty to admit that he is stealing
from the Church. But is such plundering really the way forward for
Western culture today? Roger Scruton thinks not. He writes of those
who roam in search of beauty, spending many hours in churches. 'Of
course, they don't steal the works of art, nor do they carry away the
bones of the local martyr. Their thieving is of the spiritual kind. They
take the fruit of pious giving, and empty it of religious sense. This
theft of other people's holiness creates more damage than physical
violence'.[15]

Free riding like this is all very well, but eventually the 'capital' is
depleted, and I am afraid I do not have de Botton's confidence in
humanity to create and sustain atheist religion. Others have tried it

---

[12] Terry Eagleton, *Reason, Faith and Revolution: Reflections on the God Debate*, Yale
University Press, New Haven, CT. and London, 2009.

[13] The subtitle of Christopher Hitchens, *God is Not Great: How Religion Poisons Everything*,
Twelve Books, New York, 2007.

[14] Alain de Botton, *Religion for Atheists: A Non-believer's Guide to the Uses of Religion*,
Hamish Hamilton, London, 2012. Simon Critchley is another leading thinker who seeks to
do without God in his *The Faith of the Faithless: Experiments in Political Theology*, Verso,
Brookyn, NY, 2012.

[15] Roger Scruton, *Gentle Regrets*, p. 57.

(Auguste Comte and Matthew Arnold come to mind) and, like their proposals, I am willing to bet de Botton's experiment runs into the sands, if it gets off the ground at all. Without God, religion loses its lifeblood.

Instead, we need to be much more aware of what the Church (and God through the Church) has offered through the ages, and offers today, to create our civilised society. Instead of stealing from churches the time has come to put something back.

So, yes, I commend the Anglican Church to a generation who think they know what they have discarded, or who have a blind spot about the Church as they discuss the way forward for society today.[16] Why the Anglican Church? Again, I hope that becomes clearer as we proceed. In England, simply, because the Church of England is the national church and continues to be a presence in the land unlike any other. It offers a natural belonging in its parochial system. But it is also present in most other countries of the world as the Anglican Communion, and as such is a significant global community. I commend it particularly because it has traditions of worship that go back centuries, with continuities as well as discontinuities with the Roman Catholic Church from which it developed. In many places today it provides the significant building that symbolises community. It also has a particular form of governance that emerged during the sixteenth and seventeenth centuries, which has much to commend it, as we shall see.

The Church of England is also, historically, the established church in England. Perhaps this is best understood today by drawing on a speech made by Queen Elizabeth II in February 2012 to mark the

---

[16] It was disappointing to read Lammy on the riots, and note that he didn't suggest that the Church upbringing he had received might have things to offer today to the young people of Tottenham. Phillip Blond lists the church, positively, alongside other civic organisations, but it is so much more, as I will argue here. Jesse Norman, as we will see, talks only of the Church as 'a religious strand'.

beginning of the celebrations of her Diamond Jubilee year. In it she
paid tribute to the nine major religious traditions represented at that
occasion, as sources of a rich cultural heritage and contemporary
families of faith. Particularly she talked of the significant position
of the Church of England, and commented that the concept of the
established Church was commonly misunderstood and, she believed,
under-appreciated in its role and duty to protect the free practice
of all faiths in this country. She stated her belief that 'gently and
assuredly, the Church of England has created an environment for
other faith communities and indeed people of no faith to live freely'.
Establishment can be understood as Christianity 'woven into the
fabric of this country' and, as such, the Church of England continues
to help to build a better society, increasingly in active cooperation for
the common good with those of other faiths.[17] A clear argument for
the role of the Church of England in today's world is made by Michael
Turnbull and Donald McFadyen. They argue for the unique place and
vocation of the Church of England and offer a confident justification
for its established role.[18]

## Being a 'vicarage'

However, their approach is rather unusual today. It is not fashionable
to credit the Anglican Church with much. It is dismissed, often.[19]
It is dismissed partly because the cultured despisers[20] of this age

---

[17] See http://www.royal.gov.uk/LatestNewsandDiary/Speechesandarticles/2012/TheQueens
speechatLambethpalace15February2012.aspx; accessed on 20 May 2012.
[18] Michael Turnbull and Donald McFadyen, *The State of the Church and the Church of the
State: Re-imagining the Church of England for our World Today*, DLT, London, 2012.
[19] See, for example, Tony Judt, *Ill Fares the Land: A Treatise on our Present Discontents*,
Allen Lane, London and New York, 2010, p. 179.
[20] The nineteenth century German theologian Friedrich Schleiermacher used this
expression as he wrote for his age.

often think they know all about Christianity, but are actually rather ignorant, *and* prejudiced against it, listing off any number of historical faults that did, or did not, happen: half truths received and believed. Like Bentley Hart,[21] who makes no apology for the failings of Christianity, and they have been many, I am not in the business here of a wholesale defence. Much rather I would like to convince my readership that Christianity, despite its fallibilities, has contributed an enormous amount to our civilisation. Certainly, the dear old Anglican Church is not very good at capturing the imagination these days. In fact, rather the opposite; it is good at being on the back foot in the media – of giving away ground that it should not. The TV programme *Rev* presents the state of play rather well: the ironies of the role, the complexities and kindnesses of being a 'vicarage'; the gentle self-deprecation; and the occasional poignant triumph (football matches and school assemblies).

*Rev* hints at the massive amount of work that parish priests do throughout the villages, towns and cities of this land that goes unsung, living out lives of public service and calling that remain true to a historical movement that has been nothing short of a revolution in civilisational terms. You see something similar in Patrick Gale's humane study of *A Perfectly Good Man*[22]; the life of a good priest with imperfections. Christians believe – and, indeed, one might argue from the simple fact of its endurance – that without the continuing sustaining and creative love of God in Jesus Christ and in the Holy Spirit, Christianity would have died long ago. Instead it has been and continues to be a revolution like no other. Bentley Hart traces this 'revolution' as he calls it, noting its great impact upon the pagan world

---

[21] See *Atheist Delusions*, passim.

[22] Patrick Gale, *A Perfectly Good Man*, Fourth Estate, London, 2012.

of Roman times and ever since.[23] In a world where, increasingly, truth is seen as relative in different cultures and times, Christians maintain that Jesus Christ showed the love and truth of God, and that love and truth need to be lived out as a way of life and service of others. True in Roman times; true, Christians claim, today.

That understanding offers a way of seeing the world and humanity that is significantly different to other world views, and it creates a different soul, and therefore a different humanity.

# A different anthropology

The secular soul has its own way of understanding of what it means to be human. From it emerges an anthropology that is different from the Christian or indeed other religious understanding. Muslims I know would like Western societies to be more confident about their Christian traditions and contemporary practice, for they know that Christians, with the imagination of faith, can have a richer understanding of humanity as a result.[24] One that is better than that of the secular humanists, for all their belief in the goodness of humanity, ethics, the rhetoric of inclusion and multi-cultural pluralism.

The secular soul is challenged here in the belief that Christianity offers much more to enable humanity to flourish: that the soul is richer, more graceful, more virtuous as a result of a turn to the traditions of religion, the fruits of which benefit a society in real need.

---

[23] *Ibid.*, Part Three.
[24] Witness the enthusiastic support that David Cameron received from Muslim leaders after his speech in December 2011, and the speech Baroness Sayeeda Warsi made in February 2012.

'*I think our world has become harder, you know.*'

*She did not want that to be true, but she thought it probably was. What had happened? Had the human soul shrunk in some way, become meaner, like a garment that has been in the wash too long and become smaller, more constraining?*[25]

---

[25] Alexander McCall Smith, *The Charming Quirks of Others*, Little, Brown, 2010, p. 111.

# 2

# *A brittle society*

The rhetoric has been of 'Broken Britain',[1] since David Cameron, the leader of the Conservative party, vowed to 'fix Britain's broken society' in *The Sun* newspaper in 2007. In the aftermath of the riots in 2011 the language re-emerged.[2] I do not think Britain is broken, but I do think it is brittle. Brittle Britain. It sounds like the words would shatter if they were to fall; spitting out through the teeth as if a series of Ts are hitting the hard ground. But brittle is not broken.

A sense of humour helps. Think of *Little Britain*, the comedy programme that ran from 2003 to 2007. With a clever title which combined Little England and Great Britain, the sketches of the show parodied the British people from all walks of life and in various familiar situations, as if a guide aimed at non-British people. *Little Britain* presented a self-deprecating irony: sardonic, edgy, willing to

---

[1] The term pioneered by the Centre for Social Justice, according to Blond, *op. cit.*, p. 74.

[2] Lammy prefers the expression 'Broken Britain' to the talk of a feral underclass that was used after the riots. At least with 'Broken Britain' it's everyone's responsibility. As soon as you describe some members of society as 'feral', you are using 'us and them' language, unhelpfully, he'd say, *op cit.*, p. 57. 'The grave danger is that the language of the "underclass" perpetuates the problem that it refers to, ghettoising a group of people by ignoring the relationship between them and the rest.'

cause offence by calling into humour the cherished and ridiculous aspects of living in Britain today.

## Little Britain; little England

Little Britain; little England. The term 'little England' was first used on 5 November 1626, by the English Puritan preacher, Thomas Hooker, as he preached a Gunpowder Day sermon. The term came into common parlance much later, though, to describe the Little Englanders who took an anti-imperialist stance during the time of the Second Boer War (1899–1901). They were against the British Empire, and for 'England', arguing that England should extend no further than the borders of the United Kingdom.

More recently, the term 'Little Englander' refers to those in contemporary society who are regarded as xenophobic and nationalistic. The English Defence League (EDL), founded in 2009, captures these sentiments. Its stated aim is to oppose the spread of Islamism, Sharia Law and Islamic extremism in England. On its website the following Government petitions are listed:

- Remove Sharia Law from the UK
- Ban halal slaughter in the UK
- Ban the Burka
- Bring our Troops home
- Ban unregulated home based Islamic learning centres.

It uses street-based marches to attract attention to its message and, in March 2010, the EDL claimed a membership of about 300 active supporters. It presents itself as multi-ethnic and multi-faith. As it says on the website:

We the English Defence League are a grass roots social movement who represent every walk of life, every race, every creed and every colour from the working class to middle England our unity and diversity is our strength.

The EDL claims to opposes only 'jihadists', but as demonstrated in London on 13 September 2009, members were heard to chant 'We hate Muslims' at pro-Palestinian demonstrators. A demonstration in Leeds in October 2009 led to stand-offs with the Unite Against Fascism group.

In 2006 I was appointed a residentiary canon at the Cathedral in Bradford, fully involved in developing connections and networks with the Asian-heritage communities of that city.[3] In 2010 the EDL said it was coming to the city-centre. The fears were real. City leaders worried that the work done in Bradford since the 2001 riots would be jeopardised by EDL activity. In fact, when the EDL descended upon Bradford in late August 2010 for a rally, the city remained resilient. They were contained and prevented from provoking a response. But the development of such groupings indicates a growing unease and vocalisation of disquiet at what is perceived to be Islamic extremism. This sort of polarisation of extremist viewpoints is one we will return to, for it is the logical outcome of the politics that can emerge from 'identity' and contributes to the brittleness of Western culture.

## The best day of my life for ever – I swear to God

In the warm afterglow of the London Olympics it's hard to remember that the riots of summer 2011 were altogether more serious in various cities of the UK. They were initially sparked by the death of Mark Duggan, shot on 4 August by the police in Tottenham, London.

---

[3] The story of much of that is told in *Fear and Friendship: Anglicans Engaging with Islam*, Frances Ward and Sarah Coakley (eds), Continuum, London, 2012.

Two days later a small demonstration, seeking information about Duggan's death and receiving an unsatisfactory response, flamed into riots and for four nights major cities and areas of cities were trashed.

The research is disturbing. In December 2011, the London School of Economics in partnership with the *Guardian* newspaper, and with support from the Joseph Rowntree Foundation and Open Society Foundations, published *Reading the Riots*.[4] A team of 30 researchers interviewed rioters from London, Liverpool, Birmingham, Nottingham, Salford and Manchester. The majority of these had rioted but had not been caught. Promised anonymity, 270 were prepared to tell their stories.

The image of two police cars burning in Tottenham circulated on mobile phones within minutes. Four days later, five people were dead, many injured, and millions of pounds worth of damage done after 15,000 people took to the streets. What motivations emerge? Hatred of the police and a sense of triumph that they could not control or stop the rioters. A desire for goods to sell on. Joining for the hell of it – 'I got the biggest adrenaline rush of my life', said one. By Monday 8 August, the rioting began in Hackney and erupted in towns and cities over Britain, much worse in scale and intensity than in 1981. The resentment against the police is palpable, as you read what the interviewees say.

> Charlie refused to say whether he fought police that night. But he described the experience as 'like a dream'. 'I was actually doing it. I felt alive, there's no word to explain it. It was like that first day it happened will always be the best day of my life for ever – I swear to God.'

Others joined in, but after a while, did not like what they were seeing.

---

[4] *Op. cit.* The Kindle Version does not have page numbers.

Simon got a good feel for Croydon. He stole a bike and cycled round before he saw a teenager with a looted iPhone4. 'I took it off him. Fresh, brand new and that's £500. Brand new out of the shop. Easy, easy quick money.'

Then he saw six people bundle a police officer down an alley. 'I think they put a T-shirt over his head and kinda dragged him down the alley and started kicking him. I was seeing him getting hit with planks of wood. I was thinking it was getting too much, these guys are going too far now.'

Resentment and hatred against the police was a prime motivation. Much of this hatred was because the police were perceived as abusive and cruel. Most interviewed had stories of previous, even childhood, incidents at the hands of the police which had left them resentful and angry, so this was payback time. David Lammy, MP for Tottenham, remembers how it was when he was a child:

The police often seemed less like protectors and more like an occupying force. Racism was rife and it was common to be stopped, searched and often humiliated. There was a real them-and-us mentality: we withdrew cooperation and they withdrew respect.[5]

Hatred at the police and poverty were the two most frequently cited reasons for the riots among those interviewed. Many of them saw the police as another gang, another racist gang. Deep ambivalence emerged among black people.

Antipathy towards police within black communities appeared to transcend generations. One young black man in Liverpool spoke of how participating in the riots was an expression of his identity:

---

[5] Lammy, *op. cit.*, p. 2.

'Grown-ups … the elders of the community … were making it known that they didn't like the police so … that made me personally feel more like yeah, I was representing them.'

The researchers concluded that race was certainly a factor in these riots, but it was not a major motivation. More obvious was just how diverse the rioters were:

One young black man who joined the melee in Tottenham described what he saw. 'Originally it started off, it was like, yet it was a group of black people … but I seen Hasidic Jews from Stamford Hill who were down there. I seen lots of white people. I seen guys from shops – Turkish, it turned out. It was like the whole neighbourhood came out. The neighbourhood knew it was all wrong. But sadly it was the neighbourhood that got trashed. They were all out in support.'

## They never had us under manners

It was the police under attack, and symbols of establishment. And the inequalities of society are felt, according to the researchers, most by those who are black or Asian.

A 21-year-old London rioter put it like this:

'We had [the police] under control. We had them under manners for once. They never had us under manners. We had them on lock. On smash. Running away from us. We weren't running from the police. They was the criminals today. We was enforcing the law. Getting them out of our town because they ain't doing nothing good anyway for no one.'

There is a very worrying inversion here, it seems to me. What is happening when a rioter claims that those who are the law have become the 'criminals'? 'We had them under manners for once'. Instead of a society based on order and justice, we begin to see power emerging as arbitrary, up-ending a flawed institution with anarchy; for who, in this rioter's mind, represents the law? The most powerful and violent?

Then there was greed for goods for free. Looting is thought to have cost the London economy alone £300 million in insurance claims. People saw it as shopping with no staff around. It was organised, targeting goods that would make a fast profit. Some talked about getting their just rewards, fuelled by resentment against a greedy society that excluded them but also, through advertising, pressured them to wear the right gear. Some took only from major retailers: Foot Locker, JD Sports, PC World, mobile phone outlets. There was real sense of euphoria: 'It was just a happy vibe'.

For others, they felt shame afterwards; a sense of having fulfilled stereotypes. Women rioted and looted in significant numbers too, sharing the hatred of the police, angry at the way in which male members of their families had been stopped and searched and treated with contempt.

To begin with, it was thought that gangs had orchestrated the riots, but subsequently that seemed not to be the case. Instead, gangs suspended their hostilities in order to join in. There were even some pleased reactions that gangs had come together against a common enemy for the duration of the riots, although old rivalries were resumed when the riots ended. Much more important as a means of organisation and coordination was the BlackBerry. Secure, cheap to run and owned by everyone, the BlackBerry summoned rioters to the latest hotspot, 'providing a roadmap to the impending disorder'.[6]

---

[6] Lammy suggests that BlackBerry should have done the responsible thing and suspended its network during the riots, *op. cit.*, p. 27.

# In this day and age you have to have money

The sense of grievance was widespread during August 2011. The grievance highlights the importance of money. A 28-year-old unemployed man in Brixton, watched a crowd of teenagers, and said:

> All these little kids ... are going to get together and they say: 'Right, you ain't got no money, I ain't got no money, we ain't got nowhere to go, no one gives a crap about us, so why are we sitting here trying to be decent people when that's not getting us nowhere?'
>
> In this day and age you have to have money. If you've not got no money then there's nothing you can do, it's even worse for you. So the first thing they're going to do is get together and find that money – somewhere, somehow.

The inequalities of wealth distribution in Britain today were cited as unjust. The lack of employment meant that many did not care. If they had a criminal record, there was no incentive to be different, as the chances of work were seen to be non-existent. But it was not just those with a criminal record. There was widespread anger at people who were grossly rich, and particularly bankers who reap massive bonuses. The researchers of *Reading the Riots* were unsure how much of this anger reflected retrospective justification for the looting and greed and how much was an honest motivation of anger at an unfair Britain. Many did not feel part of Britain: 51% of those interviewed said they did not, which contrasts with the 92% of the population as a whole who do feel a sense of belonging. Four-fifths of those interviewed were aged 24 or under, and most expressed a profound sense of alienation from British society. Most thought that the riots would happen again.

The appeal by Tariq Jahan after the death of his son in Birmingham made a big impact and, according to the researchers, certainly helped to bring the rioting to an end. This was a remarkable intervention by a brave man, which recalled people to a sense of normal order. His words had the transformative effect of reversing the inversion of law and criminal.

## What kind of life it is

David Lammy was shocked by footage. He expected to see faces full of rage and resentment at the death of Mark Duggan. But 'the video depicted a far more sinister emotion: happiness ... plenty of what went on was not spontaneous and unthinking – it was cruel and calculating.'[7]

In *Reading the Riots*, Rowan Williams, the Archbishop of Canterbury, stressed the importance of tackling the political issues, among which he noted unstable family settings, education delivered in almost impossible conditions, constant suspicion and discrimination, all of which led to the destructive and chaotic release of tension. He remarks:

> We may well wince when some describe how the riots brought them a feeling of intense joy, liberation, power. But we have to ask what kind of life it is in which your emotional highs come from watching a shop torched or a policeman hit by a brick.

Williams stresses that young people need love. They need a dependable background for their lives, emotionally and socially; a background that helps them take certain things for granted so that they know they do not have to fight ceaselessly for recognition.

> We should be keeping a sharp eye on working practices that undermine this, and asking how law and society reinforce the right kinds of family stability by training in parenting skills as well as high quality out-of-school activity and care. We should be

---

[7] Lammy, *op. cit.*, pp. 13–14.

challenging an educational philosophy too absorbed in meeting targets to shape character. And we should look long and hard at the assumptions we breed into our children about acquisition and individual material profit.

He argues for greater support for the teaching profession and their work to create environments where 'character is shaped and imagination nourished'. He wants to see an education system where 'we not only raise aspirations but also offer some of the tools to cope with disappointment and failure in a mature way – an education of the emotions is badly needed in a culture of often vacuous aspiration'. We shall return to this.

This is a brittle, inflammatory Britain, with a significant section of the population severely disaffected and resentful, alienated from society, and full of grievance at authority figures such as the police. People motivated by materialistic acquisition and let down by an education system that is too preoccupied by targets and measurable attainment at the expense of an emotional and moral knowledge that can shape character. Williams' analysis is right, it seems to me.

# Cultural impoverishment

David Lammy MP describes the riots as 'an explosion of hedonism and nihilism'.[8] We need to look at why so many turned out onto Britain's streets to create mayhem, with what amounted to naked amorality and a brutal lack of civilisation. David Bentley Hart in his *Atheist Delusions* argues that Christianity has offered, through the centuries, a deeply civilising impulse. Without Christianity, he asserts, society becomes

---

[8]  Lammy, *op. cit.*, p. 17.

uncivilised, with Christianity we become culturally enriched. '[A] civilised and a safe society must be policed not just by uniformed officers, but also by notions of pride, shame, self-restraint and responsibility to others', says David Lammy.[9] Such virtues grow through educative processes that are steeped in virtues that Christianity holds dear, and which help to tackle cultural impoverishment.

Cultural impoverishment is a recurring theme through this book.[10] Mainly in Western societies we understand poverty exclusively as a material concept, measured by how much money you have, or have not got. It is that, of course.[11] But it is not only that, as Frank Field has explored in his insightful report on poverty, *The Foundation Years*.[12]

Poverty is also the experience that children have when they are deprived of a real engagement with cultural goods that can give them

---

[9] *Ibid.*, p. 29.

[10] He can be rather strong meat, but Theodore Dalrymple writes from long years of experience as a psychiatrist working with what he calls 'the underclass', which is not at all the same as the traditional understanding of 'the working class'. Two books are worth dipping into for a sober assessment of the sort of cultural poverty that he says is the result of an undiscriminating welfare state, and is the worst excesses of what I'm exploring here. In *Life at the Bottom*, Ivan R. Dee, Chicago, IL, 2001, he addresses the question 'What is poverty?' (pp. 134–43). Comparing times when he has worked in Tanzania and Nigeria, and after conversations with medical colleagues from other parts of the world, he concludes 'Yet nothing I saw – neither the poverty nor the overt oppression – ever had the same devastating effect on the human personality as the undiscriminating welfare state. I never saw the loss of dignity, the self-centredness, the spiritual and emotional vacuity, or the sheer ignorance of how to live that I see daily in England. In a kind of pincer movement, therefore, I and the doctors from India and the Philippines have come to the same terrible conclusion: that the worst poverty is in England – and it is not material poverty but the poverty of the soul' (p. 143). See also his *Our Culture, What's Left of It: The Mandarins and the Masses*, Ivan R. Dee, Chicago, IL, 2005.

[11] Lammy's conversation with Gordon Brown is instructive, reported in *Out of the Ashes*. When he asked the then Prime Minister what he could do to support single mothers in his constituency as they worried about their children becoming involved in knife crime, 'Gordon looked at me quizzically while I spoke, as if I was missing something obvious. "Tax credits," he responded, as soon as I finished. "If they're single parents and they're working, they'll be entitled to them"', *op cit.*, p. 30.

[12] Frank Field, *The Foundation Years: preventing poor children becoming poor adults*, H.M. Government, London 2010.

emotional resources and moral knowledge to help them grow into adulthood and lead fulfilling lives. These cultural goods enable the development of a sense of character and resilience so that, for example, they are more able to discern when they are being seduced by markets that manipulate their desires, or detect if they are being drawn into wrong ways of behaving, or how to recognise when they are being narcissistic. Education, with this aim, shapes their personalities to the good, helping them learn to be kind, loving and able to forgive when they are hurt. It can enable them to cope with failure, and so grow into maturity. It encourages patience and self-control instead of the resentment and grievance that is so often the brittle mindset of today's Western culture. Such cultures are fortunate, though, in the extremely rich cultural heritages they have to draw upon, rich resources to enable the emotional and moral knowledge required to face the complexities of contemporary life.

There are many ways in which cultural impoverishment can be addressed. Team sports, for a start; where it takes perseverance and even painful effort to play well (or even badly) but where each offers their distinctive contribution to the team. The potential legacy of the 2012 Olympics could prove extremely important here. Or a choir, attending on a regular basis to sing, in the knowledge that the whole is impoverished by your absence, so you turn up even when you would rather watch the TV. Or unfashionable things, such as the Sea Cadets or the Girl Guides. Essentially purposeless activity (in terms of a utilitarian, purpose-driven society) that has tremendous benefits as the human person grows and develops into emotional and moral maturity, with a sense of meaning to their lives.[13]

---

[13] *Ibid.*, p. 134: Lammy writes that Modern Britain needs more institutions on the lines of the Scouts, the Girl Guides or the Boys' Brigade to ground youngsters in the habits of citizenship. No longer should we shy away from a universal civic service, helping out in schools, mentoring younger children and renovating public spaces.

Education can provide an emotional and moral maturity through a good and sound introduction to what it means to be a responsible human being. The human person flourishes best when individualism is not the over-riding value, but where each pupil knows they are part of a whole, and that it is up to them to contribute of their best. For a number of decades now, the expression 'child-centred education' has been in the foreground. It stresses that each child matters, and that care is needed to allow the child to develop as an autonomous being with his or her own individual needs. But there is a shadow here, I think. For in putting the child, or the student, at the centre of things, I wonder if we haven't encouraged an implicit self-centredness and a sense that education is a possession: a means to a rather narrow end. When the individual child is at the centre of his own educational experience, which becomes measured by targets and tick boxes, the world around him is in danger of shrinking to his limited horizons, rather than expanding to encompass unimaginable experience. Instead education should be seen as a unique gift that enables individuals to take part in something bigger than themselves, losing a sense of 'me, myself, I' in a rich heritage of learning and knowledge, an exciting adventure, well worth the effort to acquire. Tennyson, in the poem *Ulysses*, captures the quest like this:

> To follow knowledge like a sinking star
> Far beyond the utmost bounds of human thought.

Education, viewed like this, becomes not the self-actualisation of the child, but the lifelong adventure of the imagination, a passion for knowledge for its own sake. Education, in this view, is not a means to an end: but an end in itself. It is not a possession, but a gift received on trust, which needs to be given in turn.[14] In the latest Church of

---

[14] My thanks are due to Tiffins Girls Grammar School, and to the headteacher, Mrs Vanessa

England report on education, there is a real recognition that Church schools offer something different to what one secondary school headteacher identifies as prevalent utilitarian and instrumental attitudes to education. For that headteacher, 'there is a clear philosophy which comes from a Christian perspective, because there is a massive pressure towards a functional and utilitarian educational philosophy. Christian understanding of educational philosophy is so important in our schools'.[15] Below we explore what that difference is in the belief that education is the best antidote to instrumental and utilitarian attitudes that shape the secular soul.

## A better education system

I want to see a better education system that does not only serve those who are materially poor but also those who are culturally impoverished by being too rich for their own good: who display their lack of morality by being too greedy, and who fail to show a sense of public service. There are those, too, who are cruel and contemptuous, both those who delight to throw fire extinguishers at police and those who do not have the character to see beyond the clothing of poverty and who make judgements that keep poor people poor and who delight in humiliating others.

The riots of 2011 were symptomatic of much that is brittle about Britain. I believe we see here the outcome of an understanding of humanity that is the product of a secular soul that has been the dominant mindset for a number of decades now, and which has shown itself woefully inadequate to sustain a good society for all.

---

Ward, for inviting me to elaborate these points at their prize giving in September 2011.
[15] *The Church School of the Future Review*, published March 2012 by the Church of England Archbishop's Council Education Department and the National Society. The Review was chaired by Priscilla Chadwick.

We need to examine more thoroughly the social imaginary that has delivered us the riots. What soul has been dominant over the last few decades? Certainly not a Christian one, I would say, for all its historic influence on our culture and civilisation. Instead society has been shaped by a secular soul which has been informed by liberal egalitarian principles. We live in a secular humanist country, and it is time to stop simply accepting that secular humanism has all the wisdom, and examine how its dominance as a mindset has contributed to the state we're in.

# 3

# *The legacy of liberal egalitarianism*

## Liberal egalitarianism

The secular soul will often look to liberal egalitarianism for its political and moral framework. The liberal egalitarian holds to a range of values that, broadly speaking, started to emerge at the Enlightenment, and are generally taken to be universal, transcending time and place. We could briefly characterise those values like this. Each individual has supreme value and should be free; the individual has natural rights, that exist independently of government and which ought to be protected; the individual should be treated fairly and equally. Toleration should be extended to everyone in matters of religion and morality.

There is nothing, on the surface of it, wrong with such values. Many of them were born during the Enlightenment, with a parentage of the Christian tradition that shaped the Church and society in a variety of ways throughout the preceding centuries. Much good has come out of the tradition of liberal egalitarianism: a real sense of justice and equality, of fairness, and the protection of rights. Society is a better place because of the advances made since the Second World War. It is simply that, good though some of the benefits have been, this dominant ideology can find itself cornered in a cul-de-sac, where some of those benefits start to bite back, like unruly teenagers.

There are a number of commentators who are increasingly critical of liberal egalitarianism. It is worth considering what they have to say in the following three areas.

## Tolerance or trust?

Tolerance is often held up as the key, positive value of a liberal egalitarian society. As we shall see below, it has its beginnings with the philosophers of the Enlightenment. If each individual tolerates others, so that all treat each other as they would want to be treated, then society becomes more tolerant.

I wonder, though, whether this is quite as straightforward as it might seem. It has the advantage of setting a low moral threshold – one to which everyone can only agree. But therein lies a danger; for, if tolerance is the dominant moral value, it becomes difficult to know what to do when one encounters behaviour that should not be tolerated. Not all people are benign; indeed it could be argued that human beings are a real mixture of good and bad, and when we choose to think that human nature is good, we can find it difficult to deal with the negative, the bad, the evil (call it what you will).

*Isabel believed in giving moral attention to everyone. This made her profoundly egalitarian, though not in the non-discriminating sense of many contemporary egalitarians, who sometimes ignore the real moral differences between people (good and evil are not the same,*

*Isabel would say). She felt uncomfortable with moral relativists and their penchant for non-judgementalism. But of course we must be judgemental, she said,* when there is something to be judged.[1]

In a culture where 'tolerance' is the key moral marker, what happens when there are things that genuinely should not be tolerated? A lack of tolerance in others (ironically)? Or the arbitrary use of power? Cruelty? Or greed? If tolerance is the core value in society, what really results is a moral vacuum that leaves it very difficult to develop a sophisticated moral response when it is necessary to do so. When one is faced with behaviour that is malicious, bad or evil, tolerance does not take you very far. Sometimes it is just not enough to describe behaviour as intolerable, or 'inappropriate', or 'unacceptable'. To do so is to avoid an issue of moral gravity: that some behaviours or attitudes are bad and wrong and need to be named as such, in an ultimate way. Cruelty is not just 'unacceptable', it is wrong. Sometimes we really do need to judge, and a nice, liberal tolerance is not sufficient. What then? The obvious recourse in a liberal egalitarian society is the courts, or you can turn to the state to legislate. But requiring the state to intervene, with regulations and legislation, does not really take us to the heart of the matter. Lammy, a Labour politician, recognises that:

My own side's response ... had exposed its limitations. Faced with the problems of an individualistic culture, we turned to government to make society more fair, safe and virtuous. The

---

[1] McCall Smith, *Friends, Lovers, Chocolate*, Little, Brown, London, 2005, p. 6. Dalrymple comes to the same conclusion: 'Experience has taught me that it is wrong and cruel to suspend judgment, that nonjudgmentalism is at best indifference to the suffering of others, at worst a disguised form of sadism. How can one respect people as members of the human race unless one holds them to a standard of conduct and truthfulness? How can people learn from experience unless they are told that they can and should change?' *op. cit.*, p. 194.

result was a blizzard of rules, regulations, targets, measurements, instructions, inspections and initiative. In government Labour passed more crime legislation in 13 years than had been seen in the whole of the previous century. A new offence was created every day for a decade. At one point the Treasury was specifying and monitoring over 600 performance indicators. A new rule or initiative was almost always the answer to every problem.[2]

If you think you have covered the risk of child abuse by providing checklists for people to tick, then often what results is a sense of 'well, we're covered then', and a subsequent negation of responsibility and a diminution of trust. Instead of trusting people, and oneself, to have a developed moral sense that has the courage to notice things that are wrong and to speak out, the responsibility is lost in a plethora of risk assessment sheets that give us the comfort that we know our own backs are covered.[3] Paradoxically, we have become a less trusting society as a result of over-legislation born of a lack of moral confidence. No longer are adults as prepared to volunteer to be leaders for child and youth groups for fear that they might be falsely accused, or simply because of the extreme amount of checks that have to be done. No longer do children automatically trust the adults around them, as normally they should. Some children take advantage of the vulnerability of adults by alleging abuse where there is none. A balance is needed. Of course, we need to be vigilant against those who would abuse. But we are in danger, as a society, of eroding the very trust upon which we depend and which children need if they are to grow into trustworthy adults. That trust, traditionally, has been carried in the institutions of society.

---

[2] Lammy, *op. cit.*, p. 20.

[3] Conversation with Peter Powell, Consultant Paediatrician and Designated Doctor for Safeguarding, NHS Suffolk.

Blond puts it like this.

It is for this reason that liberalism has promoted a radical individualism which, in trashing the supposed despotism of custom and tradition concerning the nature of true human flourishing, has produced a vacated, empty self that believes in no common values or inherited creeds. But in creating this purely subjective being, liberalism has also created a new and wholly terrifying tyranny ... By making everyone instead the same sort of individual with basic physical needs and rights, an excess of centralised authority is required. The rule of virtuous persons is displaced by the explicit control of a central state, which has a monopoly on the use of violence and must endlessly police, through more or less subtle modes of coercion, both the sanctity of contract and the ways in which one free individual may impinge on the liberties of others.[4]

Tolerance is too passive, too laissez faire. Trust is much more morally active and engaged, and partly that trust must be in oneself to make moral judgements where necessary. Carefully, of course, and with proper discernment, but with moral courage.

The tragedy is when those very traditional institutions that should be absolutely above blame are themselves corrupt. Instead of carrying good, trustworthy virtues through time, which can be relied upon, some institutions pass on abusive practices and destroy trust where it should be most secure. Re-establishing cultures of trust and virtue is enormously difficult but necessary, whether in the police or in the Church. But because some institutions go bad, it does not mean that all institutions should be written off. Indeed, good, resilient trustworthy institutions are essential to healthy civic society, and

---

[4] Blond, *op. cit.*, p. 145.

those who carry public office within them need to be aware of what they represent, over and above their personal wants and desires. The expectation of moral rectitude should be met.

# Rights and resentments

The liberal egalitarian understanding of society starts with equal individuals, who contract with other individuals, and so society is formed. It seems obvious, and straightforward, until you start to push a little. For example, when people grow up thinking that society owes them certain rights, or when they develop a sense of identity that means they think of themselves as disadvantaged when compared with other 'identities', then very quickly a sense of victimhood can develop, and they can start to blame others or society when things go wrong. No sense of personal responsibility has been developed, so it is never their fault. This sort of victim mentality can be fed by a sense of grievance that becomes a default mindset, and the easiest way to express that grievance is with the language of rights. Lammy questions the way in which the language of 'rights' is used today.

> The problem in Britain is not that we have too many rights. It is that we lean too heavily on them as a solution to every problem. Too often we reach for a legal fix to problems that are social and cultural. Our relationships with one another become adversarial and uncompromising. We lose a sense of decency. We justify being rude or inconsiderate because we have the right to free speech. ... Our rights talk has led to a politics with too limited a vocabulary, too few ways of finding shared solutions to shared dilemmas. In a more fragmented society, much less concerned with custom and heritage, the rights reflex is tempting. ... A decent society is not

just liberated by rights and freedoms but also nourished by a sense of respect and responsibility that holds us mutually accountable.[5]

Zygmunt Bauman explored this discourse of 'rights' further in the Joseph Rowntree Report on *Contemporary Social Evils*. In Western culture individuals are led to believe that each 'has the right' to consider herself equal to everyone else. However, she soon learns that she is not equal: there are people who are greater and lesser than her – in all sorts of ways: more beautiful, less intelligent, poorer, more friendly, healthier, less patient. Bauman argues that in a society where worth is measured primarily in materialist terms, then that sense of 'equality' can quickly turn sour, fostering resentment against those who have more material goods.

The issue, it seems to me, is with the notion of 'equality'. I would suggest that the concept gains its real meaning theologically. This way of thinking sees everyone equal in the sight of God, regardless of their personal circumstances. Without that theological meaning, the concept becomes empty, and fails to work in a non-totalitarian society where human differences are valued and where talent and enterprise are encouraged. If we are falsely led to believe that we are equal, but if our worth depends upon successfully competing in a society of consumers, then those who do less well become ever more resentful and full of grievance. With such an empty liberal subject as the basic building block of society, we are a far cry from the Christian conception of a society which is based upon public service and equal and impartial love of neighbours, regardless of their worth. Bauman comments that now in society, 'we would seldom be willing to accept even a minor personal inconvenience to renounce the lifestyle of consumerist indulgence.'[6]

---

[5] Lammy, *op. cit.*, p. 159.

[6] Bauman in the Joseph Rowntree Foundation report, *Contemporary Social Evils*, *op. cit.*, p. 153.

So the egalitarian value of 'equality' has resulted merely in individual competition for material goods, and, perversely, in a sense of inequality and resentment. More than that, Bauman and others draw attention to the narcissism that takes hold, where people come to perceive the world through the prism of their own self-absorption. Such people are haunted by anxiety and are forever seeking attention, affirmation or adulation. Their narcissism lays them open to manipulation, too, for any number of markets can be created to supply their insatiable desires; wants and needs, largely shaped by celebrity culture.

> *Isabel gazed at the painting of the good, and then looked at the painting of the proud. In an earlier age, it might have been possible to believe that goodness would prevail over pride, but not any more. The proud man could be proud with impunity, because there was nobody to contradict him in his pride and because narcissism was no longer considered a vice. That was what the whole cult of celebrity was about, she thought; and we feted these people and fed their vanity.*[7]

Bauman describes an absence of society as a 'form of life of the liquid-modern, thoroughly individualised society of consumers'[8] who are largely motivated by a sense of grudge and resentment for what they have not. Marr describes the same thing when he talks of 'The Democracy of Narcissism' as a mass consumer culture, where people understand equality as equal rights to consume.[9] Frustration and resentment result. Stir in 'violence glamorised on TV, on games consoles and in music, where the intricacies of human pursuit are

---

[7] McCall Smith, *Friends, Lovers, Chocolate*, p. 83.

[8] Bauman, *op cit.*, p. 156.

[9] 'First time round, of course, it was fresher. Pioneers have an innocence their imitators lack. Sixties culture was made by people who had no idea they were setting patterns for the future.' Andrew Marr, *A History of Modern Britain*, Macmillan, London, 2007, p. 263.

boiled down to "Get rich or die trying"[10] and British society has a toxic cultural cocktail that fuelled the riots and will fuel them again.

## Resentment and repudiation

I know there have been times in my life when feminism has given me a lens to understand all that was wrong with my life. It was patriarchy to blame. I was a victim, of course; done down by the patriarchal structures of society. And, yes, to some extent, it was true: I have been treated unfairly because of gender in the past. I call myself a feminist, and I welcome the way the law is there to guard against negative discrimination. It is simply when it becomes the only ideological frame in use that it starts to distort. I have fallen into the trap of blaming others, and letting myself off the hook of taking personal responsibility for myself and my actions. Because sometimes the fact I did not get the job had nothing to do with my gender. It was simply that I was not good enough, or had not prepared well enough. I have needed to 'man up' to that; and to develop some character that meant I could cope with failure, and take responsibility when it was my fault, and forgive when it was not.

A more corrosive aspect of the same resentment is described by Lammy. He describes the impact that some aspects of rap culture can have on young people, particularly black girls and boys. He sees a sinister strand of rap music that reproduces a narrative of dispossession and nihilism. It sends out the message that the system is rigged against them. If they start with low expectations, then these are reinforced. Respect and success can only be won through fear, or through hustling and criminality.[11]

---

[10] Lammy, *op. cit.*, p. 33.
[11] *Ibid.*, pp. 193–4.

When one's 'identity' as a woman or a black girl's 'identity' becomes a dominant perspective, an immediate sense of solidarity with others can result. This phenomenon is called 'identity politics', where political positions are taken and defended on the basis of identity.[12] We will return to this below, as I explore further the implications of thinking of the human person in terms of identity, rather than character and virtue. But we go another step here, for a culture in which resentment is endemic can also be a culture of repudiation.

Isabel is reviewing an article sent to her for publication in the *Review of Applied Ethics*, the journal she edits.

*That particular department of philosophy was known for its ideological position; one could not even get an interview for a job, let alone a job, unless one adopted a radical position. This poor man was uttering the shibboleths, but his heart was obviously not in them: he was a secret conservative! In this paper he had argued against the family, calling it a threat to individual autonomy, a repressive institution. That was the party line, but he probably loved his family and believed that the best way of growing up adjusted and happy was to have a mother and a father. But that was heresy in certain circles, and very unfashionable.*[13]

Liberal egalitarianism has become so dominant and so much

---

[12] Beattie says this of identity politics: 'Postmodernism creates a forum in which individuals and minority groups can claim rights to self-expression and self-determination rooted in particular identities and cultural narratives which are not accountable to the judgement of outsiders. In the case of Western individualism, postmodernism privileges the here and now over the bonds of tradition, history and community. It allows for an experimental lifestyle through the expression of multiple identities – a sort of metropolitan fancy-dress parade where we act out fictional identities because there is no such thing as the "I" based on the idea of a gendered, communal, historical self with a fixed identity', *The New Atheists: The Twilight of Reason and the War on Religion*, Darton Longman and Todd, London, 2007, p. 133.

[13] McCall Smith, *The Careful Use of Compliments*, Little, Brown, London, 2007, p. 69.

part of our contemporary mindset that we can feel a conscious or unconscious pressure to conform to it as the prevailing ideology. I remember once introducing my husband to a Roman Catholic parish priest as 'my partner'. We were at a party where that was the acceptable terminology. Both Peter and the parish priest laughed at me. Such repudiation of traditional institutions most readily emerges with marriage, as Isabel recognised. Phillip Blond sees the same pressure. He describes in *Red Tory* the devastating effect that the last few decades have seen on the traditional institution of marriage.

> Year on year, the number of people who choose to marry has declined, from 415,000 in 1970 to 284,000 in 2007. While divorce rates have stabilised, with 12 married persons per 1,000 getting divorced in 2006, this is offset by a low marriage rate and a steep rise in cohabiting partnerships, half of which break up before their first child's fifth birthday. This has led to rises in the proportion of children born outside of marriage, increasing steadily from 37% in 1997 to 44% in 2007 (a rate which did not exceed 10% until the 1960s) and the proportion of children living in lone-parent families, which more than tripled between 1972 and 2006 to 24%.
>
> These are serious and unprecedented changes in what should be the most important and enduring relationships in our lives – relationships which shape our existence from childhood, giving us values and identity, guiding our decisions and forming our arche- types for further relationships; relationships which for previous generations would have extended through old age and infirmity.[14]

He argues that there is a culture of repudiation of such things as family life, but also other forms of institutional life, and it springs from that dominant liberal egalitarianism. We have seen

---

[14] Blond, *op. cit.*, p. 73.

how some institutions have undermined the trust that should be theirs, and how devastating this is to society. But institutional life is fundamental to a healthy society, and such trust needs to be regained, so that values and virtues can again be passed down, and learned from one generation to another. Repudiation of such institutional life is not the answer, especially when it is the result of an ideological fashion.

Blond has obviously experienced university departments where such a culture of repudiation holds sway.

> Unfortunately, all too many British students, who have suffered the misfortune of ten weeks of bad French philosophy, or empiricistic analytic philosophy of a more homegrown kind, emerge from university with the deep and abiding conviction that there is no such thing as objective truth and that everything cultural is arbitrary. They carry into their twenties and beyond the view that any claim about truth is hierarchical and therefore synonymous with fascism and all manner of evil and conservative consequences. ... While the idea of a universal relativism doesn't survive the first brush with serious rational reflection, such juvenile dictums have permeated our governing elite and undermined the foundations of all our great institutions.[15]

Scruton has observed something similar, but takes the analysis of this phenomenon of 'repudiation' deeper. He discusses the difference between culture and civilisation in his *Modern Culture*, and argues that the civilisation we know has gradually lost its Judaeo-Christian cultural heart. Institutional life, which once was shaped and sustained by that culture, is increasingly empty. That means we have lost the institutional continuity, largely carried in family life, but, not only

---

[15] *Ibid.*, pp. 140–1.

there, to pass on to successive generations the wisdom and character that enables young people to enter the adult world with an emotional and moral maturity, able to cope responsibly with the vicissitudes of life. It was largely carried in the aesthetic legacy of Christian belief, in art and poetry, literature, sculpture and music – all informed and undergirded by Christian belief. Because the world no longer endorses that inheritance, and because that is felt as a loss, it is repudiated, often with some force, as are the institutions that carry forward that different vision of human life to that of the liberationist philosophies of post-modern times.[16]

Now, Scruton is largely right, here. He explains the vehemence of this repudiation as an unconscious denial of the Judaeo-Christian heritage and an angry grief reaction to the emptiness that is perceived to be at the heart of culture today. Scruton offers an adequate explanation for the vehement snarls that so immediately are the response to any questioning of that egalitarian liberal ideology. Just try and question what 'equality' means in some circles. No debate will ensue, but only repudiation of the question. It is very difficult to get any rational discussion on the topic, and for years I simply agreed with that ideology, and kept such questions to myself. No longer. There is too much at stake.

## A heart beating

*'Enlightenment values? Defend those?'*

*Jane nodded. 'Probably. Because if we don't, then all is lost. Hobbes's nightmare.'*

*'Of course.'*

---

[16] Roger Scruton, *Modern Culture*, Continuum, London and New York, 2nd Edn, 2000, pp. 132–3.

'Self-interest, naked materialism, authoritarian government: all of these are alive and kicking in the undergrowth, ready to take over, ready to fill the vacuum created by the decline of Christianity.'

The mention of religion struck out. The laicisation of conversation – even about major things – had been so complete that religious references seemed inappropriate, almost gauche. And yet that was what had made us, thought Isabel. That had been at the heart of our culture; it had given our society its fundamental outlook. And could the Enlightenment have flourished in quite the same way in the absence of Christian sentiments of love and cherishing of others? Society may be post-Christian, but could hardly ignore its Judeo-Christian past; we did not, after all, come from nowhere.

'I know this is a bit blunt,' Isabel said, 'but do you mind my asking whether you have a particular religious position?'

Jane looked at her directly. 'Because I mentioned Christianity?'

'Not just that –'

Jane cut her short. 'I sometimes envy those who have a strong faith. But in answer to your question, no, I can't believe.'

'So you're like most of us today,' said Isabel. 'I have misgivings about people not having a spiritual life. It's so … shallow. I sometimes think that life without a spiritual dimension must be like being made of cardboard – and as deep and satisfying.'

She paused. 'I feel that there is something there – some force, or truth, perhaps – to put it at its most general. I sense it, and I suppose I'd even go so far as to say that I yearn for it. I want it to be. Maybe that's God. But I find it difficult to accept any statement as to his identity. And as for claims to be the sole interpreter of that force – the sort of claim made by religions that tell you that they have the sole answer – well, what can one say about such arrogance …'

'Yet you say that we need religious belief?'

Isabel did not answer immediately. The problem for her was

*the divisiveness of religion; its magical thinking; its frequent sheer nastiness. Yet all of that existed side by side with exactly that spirituality that she felt we could not do without; that feeling of awe, of immanence, which she knew was very real, and which enriched and sustained our lives so vitally.*

*'Yes, we need it,' Isabel eventually replied. 'Because otherwise we live in a world where there is no real answer to evil.'*[17]

## Christian foundations

It does not need reiterating that Western society has Judaeo-Christian foundations. The ways in which those foundations have secured society are complex, but I think partly they can be teased out in three directions.

First, Christianity has given, through the centuries, a long tradition of political thought, which enables us to think of society as a body in a particular way. On the night before he died, Jesus took bread and wine, and told his disciples that these very ordinary material substances were his body and his blood, and that they were to eat and drink them in remembrance of him. The idea of the body as a way of understanding human togetherness took on particular vitality with this action of Christ, especially when it is seen as a sacrament, an action of the Church in which God's grace, or active love, is present, transforming human existence. A gathering of people from all walks of life become one body when they receive the sacrament of the Body and Blood of Christ. Society – the political – can be understood to begin here, as the body comes together, as the corporate is created. This idea has had enormous influence, as we shall see below, on the development of Western society.

17 Alexander McCall Smith, *The Forgotten Affairs of Youth*, Little, Brown, London, 2011, pp. 35–6.

Second is the aesthetic, which enables a moral and emotional growth to occur, and here the central images of Christianity which recall the birth, life, death and resurrection of Jesus Christ offer a narrative that deepens understanding of the experience of human existence. You will see the urge to find redemption through suffering and beyond, for example, informing the best storylines of drama, poetry, literature and art within that Christian heritage, even today, even despite the dominance of secular humanism. Such art has a civilising effect, promoting a moral and emotional knowledge that provides resources for people to cope with the suffering, the pain and the joys of their lives. And to resist evil, for to recognise that God was revealed in Jesus Christ offers a model of a morality of self-sacrifice and love of neighbour.

Third, Christianity has provided a moral compass to both individuals and to society with what are called the two great commandments: to love God and to love one's neighbour. That morality has been deeply rooted in society, shaping a notion of public service that can still be identified in politics, the health service, education, the legal system and in civil society. The injunction to love God and neighbour has encouraged the disciplines of character and virtue, leading people to go the extra mile to help others, often against their own self-interest, and so growing with a more humane soul.

The political, aesthetic and moral are three foundation stones of society, giving us the Judaeo-Christian heritage that has shaped political life and culture through the centuries. When we reflect upon cultural forms that do not reflect that Christian story any more, it could be argued that we witness there a return to a Hobbesian state, for instance, in many violent computer games, where self-interest rules and barbarity starts to take hold. And perhaps it could be said that much so-called post-modern art merely reveals a vacuum at its heart in its very triviality and narcissism; a nihilistic vacuum shaped around the felt loss of the profundity of the Christian story. And, of course, the so-called 'playfulness' and 'irony' of much contemporary post-modern art and architecture only works, ultimately, when that serious story is there, even in its absence.

The repudiation of the Christian 'grand narrative' of resurrection – of the truth of a life that triumphs over evil and death – leaves us merely with human existence in a material world, bereaved, with imaginations impoverished, and no longer able to consider the possibility that there might be more to life than what is reflected back to us from the acres of glass of so much post-modern architecture. We have to fall back on human nature as we find it, or seek to create it beyond good and evil, without any transcendent reference that has goodness and love at its heart. Things must be reduced to material. Poverty becomes a material matter: a lack of material goods, rather than a lack of cultural resources. We become ever more culturally impoverished, unable to know or to shape future generations in anything other than material and measurable ways. In a material world, we become ever more materialistic, because there is no alternative way to value meaning. Without the God of Judaeo-Christianity, who gives us a sense of the law, of right and wrong, of love and justice, of equality, of mercy and truth, from beyond human experience, I would argue that there is not enough to build society upon.[18]

## The secular soul doesn't work

*Les Philosophes* – Hobbes, Locke, Rousseau amongst them – had the luxury of living in societies that continued to draw their lifeblood from centuries of Christian political thought and habit. Their thought experiments have given us societies which no longer draw on that

---

[18]  For further reading, see Scruton, *The Face of God, op. cit.*

lifeblood. And as that Judaeo-Christian heritage becomes weaker, the fabric of society starts to unravel.

The individual forgets how to be corporate. The individual starts to treat others with their own self-interest foremost, tolerating the self-interested motivations of others (in so far as they do not conflict, and confused when they do), and this basic moral assumption replaces the Christian injunction to love one's neighbour and to put the needs of others above one's own. We become ever more utilitarian and instrumental in our dealings, and we forget how to do things, and be with people, for their own sake, as ends, who point to other ends beyond themselves. We become shallow identities, without the corporate knowledge around us to form character and to be virtuous.

To be provocative, I would say that the secular soul creates a mindset that is disastrous for human society, significantly responsible for the brittle state that many western societies find themselves in.

# Part Two

# 4

# *Such a thing as society*

## A romantic notion

We have begun to explore how certain political theories emerged during the Enlightenment, which shuffled off the shackles of traditional authorities (such as the Church). Various philosophers, most notably Hobbes, Locke and Rousseau, went back to basics, and imagined what the original state of human nature was, before society formed. Hobbes argued for a social contract between people, and he also thought that it was necessary for the people to set up a sovereign power, which could be embodied in one person or in an assembly, to enforce the contract and make law. The social contract bound human individuals into society, saving them from their brutal selves, and civilising them into mutual regard. Locke, too, proposed that the transition from the state of nature to civil society required a social contract, whereby free individuals contracted together to accept the curtailment of their freedom in exchange for the mutual benefits and securities of society.

These social contract theories have highly influenced popular views of democracy today.[1] Rousseau was another thinker who

---

[1] There is, however, a deep flaw in such theories. You need some sense of civil and moral liberty to make a contract in the first place: 'how can society be founded on a contract,

attempted, in 1762, to outline the contractual processes that create a society. I focus particularly on him because he differed from Hobbes in one key respect. Rousseau thought that humanity in its primordial state was not self-interested and warring, but benign and compassionate, and as a result he has a greater hold on the secular soul of our current social imaginary, which tends to think of humanity as naturally good.

Rousseau argued, as we shall see, that good human beings come together to form society for their own benefit, but then that very society starts to trap and constrain them. 'Human beings are born free but are everywhere in chains', he cried: they need to be free to realise their true, good nature; free to seek the expression and realisation of self that is the authentic life.

Rousseau has, justifiably, been called the Father of Romanticism. The conception of the human being as free and expressive captured the imagination of Europe from the eighteenth century onwards. You can detect romanticism in many different art forms, leading up to the Modernist Movement of the twentieth century. The romantic who seeks self-fulfilment emerged powerfully and popularly as the zeitgeist of the 1960s and 1970s. Freedom became freedom from constraint, freedom to be by throwing off the dead weight of tradition and responsibility. Some commentators now look at that concept of freedom, and wonder if it is as innocent as it seems.

David Lammy, examining the causes of the 2011 riots, identifies two revolutions in recent Britain.

---

when no contract can exist until society has been founded?' asks Scruton in his essay 'Rousseau and the Origins of Liberalism', in Mark Dooley (ed.), *The Scruton Reader*, London and New York, Continuum, 2008, p. 45. Those interested in reading further, and from a sympathetic perspective, on Jean-Jacques Rousseau, should read Simon Critchley's *The Faith of the Faithless, op cit.*, particularly Chapter 2, 'The Catechism of the Citizen'.

The first was social and cultural: the social liberalism of the 1960s. The second was economic: the free market, liberal revolution of the 1980s. Together they made Britain a wealthier and more tolerant nation. But they have come at a cost, combining to create a hyper-individualistic culture, in which we do not treat each other well.[2]

These two revolutions were built around notions of personal freedom that came from Rousseau, but, says Lammy, at what cost?

The riots were a reminder that, whether we like it or not, we are heavily dependent on one another. We are not born free, as we like to believe, but dependent on our parents. As we grow older, a good life depends in large part on the strength of our relationships with family, friends, neighbours, colleagues and strangers. It is contingent on a society characterised not just by liberty but by mutual respect and mutual responsibility. When this breaks down it takes a lot more than police officers to put things right.[3]

When, in the 1960s and 1970s, the authority of parents was questioned, you can look straight to Rousseau, for it was he that said:

The oldest of all societies, and the only natural one, is that of the family; yet children remain tied to their father by nature only so long as they need him for their preservation. As soon as this need ends, the natural bond is dissolved. Once the children are freed from the obedience they owe their father, and the father is freed from his responsibilities towards them, both parties equally regain their independence.[4]

---

[2] Lammy, *op. cit.*, p. 17.
[3] *Ibid.*, p. 19.
[4] Jean-Jacques Rousseau, *The Social Contract*, translated and introduced by Maurice

'Doing your own thing' became the dominant theme of a couple of decades that dismissed the strictures of parents' generation. Excessive individualism was born then, in the sense that it truly came into its own, as Jose Harris[5] and Tony Judt[6] have described.

Margaret Thatcher's economic policies dovetailed nicely with that excessive individualism, and the wind was set fair for the 1980s, a decade of unprecedented licence, and greedy people making good. We reap the whirlwind today.

## '... no such thing as society'

Politically and economically, it suited the neo-liberalist approach of Margaret Thatcher to re-conceptualise the relationship between the individual and the state, as many have identified. The actual text of Thatcher's famous 'no such thing as society' interview with *Women's Own* in 1987 does not support the claims that are often made of it: that she was opposed to all forms of social and collective action. But the British mindset did change when she was in power,[7] and her neo-liberal monetarist policies have made an impact upon how we view ourselves as human beings.

Thatcher was very influenced by the Austrian economist, Friedrich Hayek.[8] Hayek had been forced into exile from Vienna by the Nazis in 1934, and he continued to worry why it was that liberal Austria had collapsed and given way to fascism. Hayek concluded that it

---

Cranston, Penguin Books, London, 1968, p. 50.

[5] Jose Harris, in *Contemporary Social Evils*, Chapter 2 '"Social evils" and "Social Problems" in Britain since 1904', pp. 5–24.

[6] See Judt, *op. cit.* for a detailed account of this change of mindset.

[7] Harris comments that 'the full impact of 'Thatcherism' on the values and structures of British society in the later twentieth century still awaits serious historical assessment', *op. cit.*, p. 16.

[8] See Judt, *op. cit.*, pp. 98–9. Blond says Milton Friedman's impact was just as great as Hayek, *op. cit.*, pp. 33–4.

was because of the shortcomings of the Left, and the best way to defend liberalism and an open society was to keep the state out of economic life. With these ideas behind Thatcher, the market was given free rein.[9] Judt argues that Blair and Brown simply continued this trajectory:

> But in the course of the Thatcher-Blair-Brown era the sanctification of bankers, brokers, traders, the new rich and anyone with access to large sums of money has led to unstinting admiration for a minimally-regulated 'finance services industry' – and a consequential faith in the naturally benevolent workings of the global market for financial products.[10]

Rousseau had believed that the human being in its natural state was good and benign, and that confidence was transferred to the workings of the market. It was 'naturally benevolent'; deregulated and left to its own devices it would 'naturally' serve the best interests of society. A deregulated market went with other things as well. Public services become privatised, welfare became increasingly means-tested, and deep-seated changes happened as a result to the traditional British way of life.[11] Jose Harris has described these changes as so profound as to alter even who the British people actually were.

> Skilled and semi-skilled industrial workers who in 1951 had made up 70% of the adult male employed population in Britain, by the end of the 20th Century accounted for little more than 15%; their successors having moved upwards into offices and professions,

---

[9] Lammy quotes Milton Friedman, another economist who influenced Margaret Thatcher: 'There is one and only one social responsibility of business – to use its resources and engage in activities designed to increase its profits' *op cit.*, p. 87.

[10] Judt, *op. cit.*, p. 104.

[11] Blond says about Blair and Brown 'on their watch poverty has concentrated, inequality has increased and social mobility is worse than it was in the 1950s', *op cit.*, p. 20.

sideways into marketing and retail or downwards into the ranks of the long-term sick and casually employed.

Such a fundamental change had a real impact upon social relations and culture because the working classes had also had a strong civil, sporting, literary and communitarian culture. Instead of workers, people became consumers 'whose main leisure activity (after watching television) was shopping'.[12]

Worker morphs into consumer. Romantic individual, throwing off the constraining chains of family and society, seeks self-fulfilment. The consumer is an easy target. And so the nice, romantic 'free spirits' of the 1960s become fodder for no, not a benign and good, but rather a cynical market, which provided any number of therapies and ointments to stroke the narcissism of a secular soul obsessed by its right to self-expression, self-realisation and 'authenticity'.[13]

There's more to say, though, as we try to understand the complexities of trends and forces that have created the brittleness of Western society in Britain and other parts of the world today.

# Homo economicus

We have seen how the worker becomes the consumer. How the romantic, flower-power individual threw off the authority of her parents, and went after self-fulfilment. We need also to note the backdrop of economic history that has viewed the human being in

---

[12] Harris, in *Contemporary Social Evils*, p. 16.

[13] Markets don't just feed the desire for self-fulfilment. Andrew Marr comments that 'Even attacks on capitalism could be marketed and sold – witness all those commercially produced Che Guevara badges and posters of Mao ... Once people had so many things they were bored of simply possessing, then capitalism would sell them experiences too, such as foreign travel and nostalgia', *op. cit.*, p. 331.

utilitarian terms. Human beings have been understood consistently by economists not as social but as economic creatures, motivated by self-interest and the desire to acquire more. Jesse Norman explores how the discipline of economics has developed in isolation from other, more rounded, understandings of society and human nature.[14] He argues that it was with utilitarian ideology that *homo economicus* began. He cites J. S. Mill who said that economic theory

> ... does not treat of the whole of man's nature as modified by the social state, nor of the whole conduct of man in society. It is concerned with him solely as a being who desires to possess wealth, and who is capable of judging of the comparative efficacy of means for obtaining that end. It predicts only such of the phenomena of the social state as take place in consequence of the pursuit of wealth. It makes entire abstraction of every other human passion or motive.[15]

Such ideas reveal the lasting impact of Jeremy Bentham, whose theories we shall come to below. Suffice to say here, economists have, almost exclusively, seen the individual as motivated by self-interest and the desire for gain. *Homo economicus* is an individual, reduced to consumer, stirred by desire for materialistic wealth.

## What is to be done?

We reap the whirlwind with the riots as the worst excesses of the Thatcher–Blair–Brown years become apparent. Two major ways forward emerge, each arguing from different points on the political spectrum.

---

[14] Jesse Norman, *The Big Society: The Anatomy of the New Politics*, University of Buckingham Press, Buckingham, 2010, p. 49.
[15] Cited by Norman, *op. cit.*, p. 54.

Tony Judt was, until his death in 2009, the University Professor and Director of the Remarque Institute at New York University. His *Ill Fares the Land: A Treatise on our Present Discontents* is wide-ranging and astute in its analysis.

In it he argues for a turn to the state. We need 'to learn to *think* the state again'.[16] During the twentieth century the state has achieved much. 'We take for granted', he says, 'the institutions, legislation, services and rights that we have inherited from the great age of 20th century reform'.[17] With a greater moral sense, a re-assertion of the innate goodness of humanity, whereby we lay aside our selfishness, we can rebuild a harmonious society, and reverse our selfish desires so that we can '... produce among mankind that harmony of sentiments and passions in which consist their whole race and propriety'.[18] Here we have it again: that unquestioning belief in humanity's innate goodness. Judt's way forward reveals his faith in humanity, and in its benevolent instincts. He has faith that humanity can reverse our selfish desires. He has no trust that religion can help this process, for 'nor can we retreat to religion: whatever we think of accounts of God's purposes and His expectations of men, the fact is that we cannot hope to rediscover the kingdom of faith. In the developed world especially, there are fewer and fewer people for whom religion is either a necessary or sufficient motive for public or private action'.[19]

I wish I was as confident as Judt is about the benevolence of humanity, and its ability to turn back the decades of self-interest we have seen since the 1960s. I think we have seen enough of a materialist, humanist era to know that it reverts rather quickly to

---

[16] Judt, *op. cit.*, p. 199, emphasis original.
[17] *Ibid.*, p. 222.
[18] Judt, *Ibid.*, citing Adam Smith, p. 187.
[19] *Ibid.*, p. 179.

a Hobbesian hell. Nor do I think the state holds the answers. Yes, the state has achieved tremendous advantages for all, particularly since the birth of the National Health Service, offering cradle-to-grave support. I think there is evidence, though, that the more needs are met, the more expectations are raised. Judt's understanding of society depends on the functions of the state, which are proving to be increasingly overstretched without some mechanism to manage the expectations upon it.

Interestingly, Judt draws on Edmund Burke, not only in the sub-title of the book, but also to back up his argument in support of the state. He says of Burke:

> Any society, he wrote in *Reflections on the Revolution in France*, which destroys the fabric of its state, must soon be 'disconnected into the dust and powder of individuality'. By eviscerating public services and reducing them to a network of farmed-out private providers, we have begun to dismantle the fabric of the state. As for the dust and powder of individuality: it resembles nothing so much as Hobbes' war of all against all, in which life for many people has once again become solitary, poor and more than a little nasty.[20]

Judt misreads Burke here. Burke did not, as Judt does, conflate the fabric of society with the fabric of its state. Burke's era was one in which the state as we know it would barely have been recognised. Instead, Burke advocated the traditions and institutions of civil and political society, such as he knew them, and, again, political society was significantly different to ours today. Burke argued that humanity is at its best when loyal to 'little platoons' of social engagement. Burke was very clear that society did not begin with the

---

[20] *Ibid.*, p. 119.

social contract theory of Locke, Hobbes and Rousseau, but rather with 'little platoons', traditional corporate associations. Without such associations, individuals become dust and powder.[21] Burke doesn't begin in the same place: his political thinking is not the same stuff as social contractual trajectory upon which Judt bases his idea of the state.

The other direction that has emerged in the last year or so picks up and develops the Cameron slogan of 'the big society'. Jesse Norman is the Member of Parliament for Hereford and South Herefordshire. He too has read his Edmund Burke, and suggests a different interpretation, one that rolls back the state, and allows a different society to emerge, drawing on 'A Conservative Ethical Tradition'.[22]

Looking back to Aristotle, he argues that virtue is acquired through custom, shaped by habit, culture and tradition. He does not go with the social contract theorists, the Hobbes–Locke–Rousseau trajectory, which he describes as '... a game-theoretic abstraction from life'. This trajectory was one which Burke attacked at 'its deepest point'.

> For Burke, as for Aristotle, man is a social animal. There can thus be no explanatory value to considering a state of nature in which man is somehow to be understood independently of society: man's natural state is civil society itself. Where Hobbes deliberately ignores trust, culture and tradition, Burke treats them as constitutive of our humanity. Where Hobbes stresses the primacy of the individual will, Burke stresses the natural reciprocity of rights and duty which occurs within society. Where Hobbes sees

---

[21] See Blond, *op. cit.*, p. 72 where he bemoans the lack in British society today of civil institutions: 'Gone is the Burkean ideal of a civic, religious, political or social middle to balance between the demands of individuals and the power accrued by the state in delivering them.'
[22] Norman, *op. cit.*, pp. 188ff.

freedom as negative, lying in the absence of constraint, Burke lays the ground for freedom as a positive value, as a capacity afforded by society for an individual to flourish. For Burke it is in the very constraining institutions of an ordered society themselves, in the 'little platoons', that freedom is to be found.[23]

Norman contrasts Burke with Hobbes here. The contrast is even more marked between Burke and Rousseau, as we will see. It is interesting, though, that both Judt and Norman are turning to Burke, albeit to different ends. Norman, unlike Judt, does see a role for religion, but it is rather thin and not really in the spirit of Burke.

## A religious strand?

Norman notes the importance of a religious framework, or 'strand' as he calls it.

*The religious strand* is grounded in Christian teaching, and naturally focuses on issues of social justice, poverty, exploitation and deprivation. It is internationalist in its concern with human beings as such, as moral agents rather than as citizens of any particular country. To greater or lesser extent, it claims knowledge of some revealed truth about human nature, and its political authority rests upon this basis. The effects of this are to give it an explicitly moral – indeed moralistic – character.[24]

Of course, any Christian leaders worth their salt will speak up, vehemently and often, on issues of social justice and morality in whatever context is appropriate. But this role of advocacy is not the only way in which religion contributes to society.

---

[23] *Ibid.*, p. 190.

[24] Norman, *ibid.*, p. 184, emphasis original.

Burke, as a thoughtful, well-read Anglican, drew on Richard Hooker. Behind Richard Hooker was a long tradition of political thinking that extended back through the Middle Ages to St Paul, who knew his Roman law. St Paul did not start, as Hobbes, Locke and Rousseau did, with the thought experiment that the individual is the basic building block of society. For St Paul it was obvious that society, the corporate – the body – came before its members. Burke's political thinking was steeped in his Christianity, and that enabled him to offer much more than a 'moralistic' strand to how society is understood. We are born into our families, said Burke, and we are born into society and so we are citizens from the start, and Christian citizens at that. Choice does not come into it. We have a moral obligation, a duty and responsibility, both within our families, and within society.[25] Burke rejected the social contract theories of his age, and particularly that of Jean-Jacques Rousseau. His conception of the relationship between Church and society is poorly served by the notion of 'a religious strand'.

Burke belongs within a rich tradition of Christian political thought that challenges the secular soul that makes Western societies so brittle. We shall return to him. But first, let us see what Rousseau was really up to.

## Born free?

A recap. With the riots of 2011, we arrive at a toxic mix of a romantic understanding of the individual, whose main, if not sole purpose in life is to seek self-fulfilment, and an economic ideology that turns

---

[25] See Russell Kirk, *Edmund Burke: A Genius Reconsidered*, the Intercollegiate Studies Institute, Wilmington, N Car., 2009, p. 179.

the individual into a consumer, and puts value on material wealth. Thatcher's neo-liberalism is important in another respect too. Not only did she disparage the 'nanny state' but she also undermined so many aspects of the traditional institutions of communitarian culture that individuals end up, paradoxically, looking to the state for what is now missing. She undermined the civil society which was so important to Burke – the institutional and professional ways in which people belong in their localities, civil organisations and the loyalties of personal association. The individual, freed from ways that constrain us by a sense of responsibility to others around us, becomes even more self-interested, competitive and caught up in materialistic ways of consuming, with desires that markets were all to ready to supply. It is an insidious trap, and one which has left us with debts that are scary, but that is another story.[26]

## The true father of the secular soul[27]

Rousseau started with a rejection of what he understood as the Church's teaching of original sin. Instead, human individuals were naturally good and compassionate. In his *Discourse on the Origin of Inequality* he wrote of pre-social 'man':

Man in a state of nature, wandering up and down the forests, without industry, without speech, and without home, an equal stranger to war and to all ties, neither standing in need of his fellow

---

[26] Told by Norman, *op. cit.*, and see particularly Chapter 1: 'The British Economy: Mirage or Miracle?'. Blond writes: 'The debt problem is so fundamental to neo-liberalism that it extends also to the state, where our financial problems are so extreme and the global system of unregulated capitalism so murky that we don't even know, as a result of the banking assets that the Treasury has underwritten, how bad our public debt really is nor how long it will take to repay it', *op. cit.*, p. 22.

[27] Scruton's essay on Rousseau is worth reading. *The Scruton Reader*, Chapter 3, pp. 43–56.

creatures nor having any desire to hurt them . . .; let us conclude that, being self-sufficient and subject to so few passions, he could have no feelings or knowledge but such as befitted his situation . . . and that his understanding made no greater progress than his vanity.[28]

Pre-social man was, however (contrary to Hobbes' view), compassionate. Compassion is the basic human disposition. 'It is this compassion that hurries us without reflection to the relief of those who are in distress: it is this which in a state of nature supplies the place of laws, morals, and virtues, with the advantage that none are tempted to disobey its gentle voice.'[29]

In this pure state of nature, human individuals are free and equal. It is only when civil society begins that Rousseau can write, as he does at the beginning of *The Social Contract* that 'Man was born free, and he is everywhere in chains'. Words that have echoed through political theory, art and culture since.

## What sort of society?

Rousseau goes on to describe and dismiss different sorts of societies and ways in which sovereign power is exercised, including those that depend on force, and those where the citizens give authority to the king and become subjects (which Hobbes had proposed). Rousseau himself commends the society where each equal individual gives their sovereignty to the community, in an original covenant which forms the body politic. This social pact means that each member of the body politic remains sovereign because each is an equal, giving equally. Rousseau describes it thus:

---

[28] Cited by Christopher D. Wraight, *Rousseau's The Social Contract: A Reader's Guide*, Continuum, London and New York, 2008, p. 12.
[29] *Ibid.*, p. 13.

Since each man gives himself to all, he gives himself to no one; and since there is no associate over whom he does not gain the same rights as others gain over him, each man recovers the equivalent of everything he loses, and in the bargain he acquires more power to preserve what he has.[30]

In this mutual covenant a republic is created, which has 'its unity, its common *ego*, its life and its will'. This state exercises sovereignty, which remains the possession of each citizen, and is exercised on behalf of the people by the people:

When it plays an active role it is the *sovereign*; and when it is compared to others of its own kind, it is a *power*. Those who are associated in it take collectively the name of a *people*, and call themselves individually *citizens*, in that they share in the sovereign power, and *subjects*, in that they put themselves under the laws of the state.[31]

The appeal of this is attractive, and one can see how influential these words were to those who struggled under absolute monarchy, particularly in France as the 18th century drew to its close. Rousseau was particularly anxious to avoid the condition of slave, forever under the despotic rule of a tyrant, and to locate sovereign power with the people themselves, as equal and free citizens, coming together to form society as a mutual collective. The sovereign power, because it belonged to everyone, could not go against, or hurt, the people 'because it is impossible for a body to wish to hurt all of its members, and ... it cannot hurt any particular member'.[32] And each individual will not want to go against the common cause, or general

---

[30] Rousseau, *op. cit.*, p. 61.
[31] *Ibid.*, p. 62, emphasis original.
[32] *Ibid.*, p. 63.

will, as Rousseau called it, because to do so would be to 'seek to enjoy the rights of a citizen without doing the duties of a subject.'[33]

If an individual did want to exercise such independence, Rousseau said – and this has proved difficult for his supporters to explain –

> it is tacitly implied in that commitment – which alone can give force to all others – that whoever refuses to obey the general will shall be constrained to do so by the whole body, which means nothing other than that he shall be forced to be free ...

*Forced* to be free? The cracks in this benign view of politics start to emerge.

And commentators have struggled since, as well, with how the General Will of the body politic is to be discerned. For it is it 'alone that can direct the forces of the state in accordance with that end which the state has been established to achieve – the common good.'[34] It is inalienable, and indivisible, and always rightful, but 'it does not follow that the deliberations of the people are always equally right.'[35] 'Individuals see the good and reject it; the public desires the good but does not see it. Both equally need guidance'. Rousseau found he needed to introduce another character onto the scene: the lawgiver.[36]

The lawgiver is a 'superior intelligence'[37] who helps society towards its goal by a system of law that serves 'two main objects, *freedom* and *equality*'.[38] Rousseau also proposes the need for an intermediary body, the government, between the people and the sovereign which can be seen as 'the institution which pulls the citizens of the state together

---

[33] *Ibid.*, p. 64.
[34] *Ibid.*, p. 69.
[35] *Ibid.*, p. 72.
[36] *Ibid.*, p. 83.
[37] *Ibid.*, p. 84.
[38] *Ibid.*, p. 96, emphasis original.

and ensures that the laws passed by the sovereign are followed'.[39] When the individual no longer feels attuned to the General Will, then the government has the task of 'forcing an individual or a group to comply with a sovereign ruling'.[40] When things go wrong, there is also the omniscient lawgiver in the wings:

> The art of the lawgiver is to know how to settle the point at which the strength and the will of the government can be combined in the proportion most beneficial to the state.[41]

We have here, then, an understanding of society where compassionate and good individuals contract together and, as they do so, sovereignty is pooled willingly by each, although each still retains that sovereignty. The General Will is created from the wills of each citizen. Government comes into being, and the lawgiver is introduced to ensure the smooth running of the affairs of state. If, however, any individual dissents, they can be forced, for their own good, to comply.

It's an idea of society that commends itself by its very simplicity. To be fair, Rousseau always thought it should be applied to small communities – and, indeed, when I lived for a while in an intentional 'alternative' community in the East End of London in the 1980s, these ideas were the ones we lived by (except we weren't forced to be free). But when it came to be adopted by the Jacobins who led the French Revolution, all sorts of flaws – dangerous flaws – came to light. Burke was the first to identify them.

Rousseau never espoused the atheism of some of the other Enlightenment *Philosophes*, but his interpretation of Christianity was

---

[39] Wraight, *op. cit.*, p. 90.
[40] *Ibid.*, p. 91.
[41] Rousseau, *op. cit.*, p. 110.

his own, leading him to convert, conveniently, to Catholicism under the patronage of Madame de Warens, and then later, returning to the Calvinist fold when he wanted, equally conveniently, to recover his rights as a citizen of Geneva in 1755. In *The Social Contract*, Rousseau advocated a civil religion (Book IV, Chapter 8), one which, unlike religion in Christian states, 'where men have never known whether they ought to obey the civil ruler or the priest'.[42] It is clear in his formula. For in this domesticated religion, no citizen has the option to obey another body, like the Church, that might demand a different loyalty. In this civil religion the key dogma is, perhaps unsurprisingly, tolerance.

> The dogmas of the civil religion must be simple and few in number, expressed precisely and without explanations or commentaries. The existence of an omnipotent, intelligent, benevolent divinity that foresees and provides; the life to come; the happiness of the just; the punishment of sinners; the sanctity of the social contract and the law – these are the positive dogmas. As for the negative dogmas, I would limit them to a single one: no intolerance. Intolerance is something which belongs to the religions we have rejected.[43]

## Rousseau's ideas alive today

The reason for exploring Rousseau's ideas here is because, more than any other of the Enlightenment *Philosophes*, he inspires the secular soul. His ideas inform the liberal egalitarianism that we have explored above, and which has real power in the popular imagination of Western culture today. Democracy, Equality, Freedom, Tolerance

---

[42] *Ibid.*, p. 179.
[43] *Ibid.*, p. 186.

are words that go unquestioned; they are taken-for-granted goods in Western society, as is the place of religion, domesticated, out of the way, and certainly out of politics. But allowed free rein, each of these goods is susceptible to a multitude of difficulties. I would go as far as to say that Rousseau's romantic notions fuelled the riots of August 2011. Rousseau's General Will, when interpreted as a form of absolute 'democracy', is too vulnerable to abuse; it too easily results in totalitarian regimes of arbitrary power. I wonder if *Animal Farm* resonated in your mind as you read my summary of his theories above.

When Rousseau died in 1778, he was buried in a tomb on the Isle des Peupliers at Ermenonville about 30 miles from Paris on the road to Soissons. Among the visitors to the grave, which quickly became a celebrity site, was Marie Antoinette 'who came with an entourage of princes and princesses and spent more than an hour under the canopy of poplars in soulful contemplation'[44] (... though not, one suspects, of the guillotine). In 1794 Rousseau's remains were transferred to the Pantheon, where he lay near his long-term philosophical antagonist, Voltaire (both rolling in their graves, away from each other, I imagine). *The Social Contract* had been banned in Geneva, his home city, but in 1794 the governing council of that city organised a procession in honour of his birthday. In Paris, at several revolutionary *fêtes*, Robespierre offered fulsome eulogies of Rousseau:

He attacked tyranny candidly, he spoke of the divinity with enthusiasm; his virile eloquence painted in flaming colours the charms of virtue ... the purity of his teaching, drawn from nature, was profoundly opposed to vice, as much as his contempt for the conniving sophists who usurped the name of philosophers

---

[44] Maurice Cranston, *The Solitary Self: Jean-Jacques Rousseau in Exile and Adversity*, Allen Lane, New York, 1997, p. 188.

brought down upon him the hatred and persecution of his rivals and false friends. Ah! If he had witnessed this revolution of which he was the precursor and which has carried him to the Pantheon, who can doubt that his generous soul would have embraced with rapture the cause of justice and equality?[45]

Copies of *The Social Contract* were carried by members of the entourage which surrounded his coffin. The book gave an intellectual basis for the Revolution. When its leaders drew up the principles for the new society, the language was drawn from *The Social Contract*:

> The law is an expression of the will of the community. All citizens have a right to concur, either personally, or by their representatives, in its formation. It should be the same to all, whether it protects or punishes ...

Robespierre went on to claim that the dictates of his Committee of Public Safety, which orchestrated the Terror, were the very embodiment of the general will.[46]

The ideas are seductive. 'Democracy' particularly so. Many on this side of the channel were supportive as the French Revolution started. But not Edmund Burke, who distrusted the way in which power could be usurped, arbitrarily, so easily. His *Reflections on the French Revolution* had a lasting impact on British constitutional history, and he deserves to be better studied today.

## Romantic hero figure

But before we move onto Burke, one further thing to say about Rousseau. We have seen that freedom was freedom from the

---

[45] *Ibid.*, p. 189.
[46] Quoted by Wraight, *op. cit.*, p. 122.

constraints of society, of family and of community. We have also touched on how he gave birth to the Romantic Movement, which has at its heart the solitary self, the artistic individual, with nothing to declare but its genius. It is a heroic figure, who haunts, and inspires, the nineteenth and twentieth centuries. Narcissistic at times, the romantic is always ready to see creative genius in the original, the novel, the modern, and to discard the constraints of tradition. Both within Christianity, and in literature, the tension has been, and continues to be, played out. Perhaps we need to give a little less oxygen to that romantic hero figure who is alive and kicking in all sorts of ways in contemporary Western culture, and respect a little more the classical, traditional and disciplined acquisition of cultural goods that nurture emotional and moral knowledge.

I have a particular distaste for the expression 'child-centredness', so you will have to forgive me if I see its roots in Rousseau's thinking. One could argue that, since the 1970s, we have adopted a romantic and rather indulgent notion of the child who is an innocent, with innate knowledge, simply waiting to discover his genius. Innocent, yes, and requiring to be free as soon as possible of the corrupting influences of the past, of parents, of society at large, and be allowed to follow her own destiny unencumbered. When education is 'child-centred', in these terms, it is there to uncover innate wisdom and enable him to find self-fulfilment. Further work is needed on how the ideology of 'child-centredness' has limited rather than expanded the horizons of generations of children since the 1970s. We have, as a society, largely forgotten the old practices of education as the acquisition of knowledge where learning by heart, or repetition of times tables is valued. Or even Latin verbs. Such things are of little worth to the child who merely has to reveal what is already there. Yes, educational theory has moved on considerably from the 1970s, leaving behind some of the more unsound thinking that informed classroom practice then, but critical research is needed to assess the impact of those decades of 'child-centred' education and how that ideology has contributed to the creation of an understanding of the human being that tends towards narcissism and atomised individualism.

## The loss of good authority

> *But that, of course, was the problem with life. We were often unsure what the rules were or where one found them, even if we knew that they existed. It would be so useful to have a large book that one could put on the table – a book entitled, quite unambiguously, The Rules. Life would be so simple if that were the case; but it never was, and even when one paged through The Rules one would find areas of ambiguity and doubt, and one's uncertainty would return. That's why, she thought, we have judges and lawyers and courts – in other words, as a Freudian might perhaps suggest, that's why we have father. But what if father went away, or said that he really didn't know about the rules and did not want to start enforcing them? The loss of good authority, Isabel thought; that's what happened then.*[47]

Rousseau was worshipped by countless adoring women. It is easy to bring a psychological interpretation to his life and writing. His mother died when he was days old; his father frittered away his livelihood and then deserted his son, who was brought up in near slavery until he too fled Geneva, and into the bosom of the first of many aristocratic female patrons. Cranston comments that the only woman he remained with was an illiterate laundry woman, Therese le Vasseur, with whom he had five children, all of whom he sent to the orphanage as soon as they were born. Diderot called it his 'Swiss

---

[47] McCall Smith, *The Charming Quirks of Others*, p. 71.

rusticity', as Rousseau would flee the *salons* to feel at home with her, a woman who remained faithful to him despite the way he treated her.[48]

Rousseau met the leading philosophers of his age, and made enemies of each one of them, including David Hume who showed him great magnanimity and generosity when Rousseau visited England in the 1760s. Rousseau's attitude could be described, justifiably, as one of resentment and grudge, always seeing himself as the victim, seeking adulation and recognition of his 'genius' without question or criticism. I would argue that alongside a naïve and ultimately dangerous conception of 'democracy', Rousseau has also bequeathed to our culture today a most unattractive 'romantic' prototype of our culture of celebrity, and its worst traits of narcissism and resentment. The father, indeed, of the secular soul.

---

[48] Cranston, introduction to *The Social Contract, op. cit.*, p. 18.

# 5

# *From generation to generation*

## Burke saw through Rousseau

Burke saw through Rousseau. They probably met briefly in London in 1766, shortly after Rousseau's arrival there in the company of David Hume (before Rousseau wrote spitefully to Hume, breaking the friendship). Burke did not take to him.

Some commentators are of the opinion that someone's personal character has no bearing on their writing; that we should not take account of Rousseau's chaotic life as we appreciate his thinking. I consider the life and thinking to be of a piece.

Certainly, when it comes to Burke, I am predisposed to like him because of the integrity and character that he displayed in his public life and service. He had independence of mind and he championed the oppressed of his day against his own self-interest. For example, he unearthed far-reaching and terrible abuses of the Indian people by the East India Company, under the leadership of the Governor General, Warren Hastings. Burke argued that Warren Hastings should be impeached for his contempt for the lives of the Indian people, and so began one of the most prolonged legal proceedings of history, lasting from 1788 to 1794. In the end Hastings was acquitted (because there was no law upon which he could be convicted), but Burke's campaign marked the end of the hegemony of the company that had exploited the people of India over decades. Burke set a precedent for probity in public life. John Morley later wrote that Burke was responsible:

> ... once for all of a moral, just, philanthropic and responsible public opinion in England with reference to India, and in so doing performed perhaps the most magnificent service that any statesman has ever had it in his power to render to humanity.[1]

In many other ways, during his life, Burke showed himself to be generous to a fault with others. He fought for those who suffered, like the Irish Catholics. He stood by the principle of doing the right thing, often to his own cost. He lost his seat as an MP for Bristol because he insisted that he was not their delegate but their representative. He was no radical, though, and was accused of being an aristocrat. He wrote this:

> If by the aristocracy, which indeed comes nearer to the point, they mean an adherence to the rich and powerful against the poor and weak, this would indeed be a very extraordinary part. I have incurred the odium of gentlemen in this House for not paying sufficient regard to men of ample property. When, indeed, the smallest rights of the poorest people in the kingdom are in question, I would set my face against any act of pride and power countenanced by the highest that are in it; and if it should come to the last extremity, and to a contest of blood – God forbid! God

---

[1] Jim McCue, *Edmund Burke and our Present Discontents*, Claridge Press, London, 1997, p. 22.

forbid! – my part is taken; I would take my fate with the poor, and low, and feeble. But if these people came to turn their liberty into a cloak for maliciousness, and to seek a privilege of exemption, not from power, but from the rules of morality and virtuous discipline, then I would join my hand to make them feel the force which a few, united in a good cause, have over a multitude of the profligate and ferocious.[2]

He was a man one would trust: well read and thoughtful, a character with principles of virtue upon which he based his public and private life, and by which 'rules of morality and virtuous discipline' he judged others. Some have accused him of inconsistency in that he supported the American Revolution, although not the French. But for Burke they were very different. He supported the American Revolution because he believed that England could not govern those colonies without their consent and will, and the King and distant parliament were over-extending their authority in trying to impose taxation and administration.

## Burke on the French Revolution

The French Revolution was different to the American, and Burke's *Reflections on the Revolution in France* of 1790 offered a clear defence of British constitutional government against the happenings in France. It must be said that Burke does not dwell at all on the abuses of the *Ancien Regime* and perhaps underestimated the blatant injustices of late eighteenth century French society. Nevertheless, in his defence of British political life he commends the importance of a

---

[2] From a speech on the bill for repeal of the Marriage Act, 1781, cited by Russell Kirk, *Edmund Burke*, pp. 79–80.

system of government which, through checks and balances, prevents the arbitrary exercise of power.

Why is this important today? Because there's no harm in reminding ourselves of how a constitutional monarchy like ours works, and what its strengths are. The most salient is that it guards well against the exercise of arbitrary power, whether held by an absolute monarch or a dictator, or, as happened in France, the arbitrary power of democracy, where all authority is 'from the people'.

Burke believed that constitutional monarchy had developed as a hereditary institution through the centuries. It had become a constitutional monarchy a century before, after a long period of experimentation: the absolute monarchy of Charles I, a civil war, Cromwell's protectorate, the restoration of monarchy in 1662, followed by the enforced exile of James II. With the invitation to William and Mary in 1688, the will and consent of the people of Britain made a positive choice for the establishment of a constitutional monarchy.

## The case for constitutional monarchs

The monarch was not elected by the people, although they did consent to it, and for Burke this was really important. The monarch's authority did not – does not – derive from the people. Ultimately, Burke argued, this authority was divine because human society organically reflected the will of God. But constitutional monarchy is not a direct theocracy, or rule by God, either, but rather a symbolic holding of authority. Charles I had been the last monarch to attempt to rule with absolute power, with divine right, as from God. His execution in 1649 had paved the way, via a civil war, and a dictatorship, for a constitutional monarchy where the monarch held authority from a source independent of the people, but which authority was curtailed by the people.

Burke argues that the Magna Carta, which he called 'our oldest reformation',[3] had started the process, when the monarch, King John, had to accept the authority of the barons. In Burke's time this had evolved, and now that authority was limited by the House of Commons, which was elected by the people (or at least, in his time, by those who owned property; now of course, by all adults who choose to vote). The monarch's power was also limited by the House of Lords, which was made up in Burke's day by hereditary peers. Burke argues that no one constitutional body could dismiss any other, and in this lies the strength of the British system, for here are checks and balances that prevent arbitrary power from taking hold in a way he observed in France.

> The House of Lords, for instance, is not morally competent to dissolve the House of Commons; no, nor even to dissolve itself, or to abdicate, if it would, its portion in the legislature of the kingdom. Though a king may abdicate for his own person, he cannot abdicate for the monarchy. By as strong, or by a stronger reason, the House of Commons cannot renounce its share of authority. The engagement and pact of society, which generally goes by the name of the constitution, forbids such invasion and such surrender. The constituent parts of a state are obliged to hold their public service with each other, and with all those who derive any serious interest under their engagements, as much as the whole state is bound to keep its faith with separate communities. Otherwise competence and powers would soon be confounded, and no law be left but the will of a prevailing force.[4]

---

[3] Edmund Burke, *Reflections on the French Revolution*, J. M. Dent, London, 1910 edition, p. 29.
[4] *Ibid.*, p. 19.

Although, today, we do not hold as a society that hereditary peers should, by right, hold seats in the House of Lords, there is a good argument against the second chamber becoming a body which is solely elected. The word 'aristocracy' (which Burke used) means rule by the best; the word 'meritocracy' (which he did not) means rule by those who, through their worth, have earned the right to offer political leadership. I would argue that the second chamber should consist of people appointed because they have proved their worth in different fields, with particular expertise or wisdom, or are there in some representative capacity, for example as faith leaders. This is a real strength of the House of Lords as it is presently constituted. To move to a wholly elected body would merely mean that its power comes from the same source as the House of Commons, resulting in an unhealthy competition between the two.

Burke suggests that each constitutive body derives its authority from a different source, and in this its strength lies. Democracy is not the only source of authority.

## Democracy is not the only source of authority

You can hear the spirit of Burke as Norman writes this:

> Power must be diffused; it must be shared and counterbalanced for a society to exist at all. The rule of law is both a prerequisite to and the specific creation of such power-sharing: institutions such as private property, or habeas corpus, or the independence of the judiciary naturally arise to protect existing freedoms and interests, and to permit new ones to develop. These institutions then serve as protectors of freedom in their turn.[5]

---

[5] Norman, *op. cit.*, p. 105.

A conservative, it has been said, is someone who recognises that institutions are wiser than individuals. Burke, arguably the first modern conservative, thought that the institutions of society are fundamental to enable individuals to flourish and to protect their freedoms. He did not hold that absolute democracy delivered the best kind of society. The trend in Britain today is taking us towards an idea of democracy that is closer to Rousseau's than Burke's, and we should be cautious, I believe, of losing confidence in the traditions of constitutional governance that have offered stability and continuity as they have evolved over centuries.

One of the unforeseen consequences of an atheist position is that it cannot recognise, in a material world, and therefore needs to deny, any other source of authority than that which comes from people. Burke's conception of society, on the other hand, is that society has developed over the centuries in accordance to a divine pattern, reflecting the goodness of God, as it seeks the best form of governance. He believed that the divine will is best represented in society when individuals dedicated their lives in public service of the common good, led in an exemplary way by the monarch. Marr writes this of Queen Elizabeth II, illustrating the deep Christian roots of the sort of monarchy we have inherited:

> She has great authority and no power. She is a brightly dressed and punctual paradox. She is the ruler who does not rule her subjects but who serves them. The ancient meaning of kingship has been flipped ... Modern constitutional monarchy does not mean subjection, the hand pressed down on an unruly nation. Instead it offers a version of freedom.[6]

---

[6] Marr, *The Diamond Queen: Elizabeth II and Her People*, Macmillan, London, 2011, p. 9.

These ideas are basic to the Christian understanding of society and the New Testament doctrine of kingship as service. Throughout the Gospels one reads that 'Jesus Christ came not to be served but to serve ...', and it is exactly here that a Christian and a secular soul will depart company. The Enlightenment relegation of religion to the private sphere, leaving public life a neutral territory, is a very different understanding to that which has informed the development of the British constitution since Burke – and indeed, as we shall see, before Burke.

Here is a clear case where an honest agnosticism would serve our constitution better than atheism, for there is a great deal at stake. Do we really want, as a nation, to move further towards democracy *a là* Rousseau, with the vulnerability that such an absolute democracy lays us open to? Or is it better to continue to support, indeed celebrate, a constitutional monarchy, which does presuppose the authority of God, and which is exercised as public service, and which has delivered continuity and stability? For we have a political system that recognises different sources of authority through the monarchy, and through our different houses of parliament, offering checks and balances that prevent the arbitrary abuse of power. But it does presuppose a divine source of authority; one which is increasingly fragile in a society in which atheist secular humanism is dominant.

Burke thought that democracy, without the checks and balances of other sources of authority, was too vulnerable to abuse, as happened with the tyranny that so quickly took over the French Revolution. The same 'democracy' was also too easily manipulated by the terrible ideologies of the twentieth century, as *Animal Farm* explores with such devastating acuity.

*Isabel understood, and the thought depressed her. She had often speculated on what it must be like to live in a rotten state, where*

*those in power and authority were corrupt and evil. Stalinist
Russia must have been like that; the Third Reich; and countless
lesser examples of tinpot dictatorships. How trapped one must feel;
how dispirited that there was nobody to assert the good. There
were courts and investigative journalists and public-spirited politicians who could be turned to, but what if one were powerless or
without much of a voice? One needed grammar, and volume, to be
heard. What if one lived in an area where the writ that ran in the
streets was that of a local gang leader? Or where, if one incurred
the disfavour of somebody powerful, a nod could arrange a nasty
accident? For many people, that was a reality: the police, the state,
could not give them real protection.*[7]

Burke, with his defence of a constitutional monarchy, limited in its
power by the authority derived both from democracy (in the House
of Commons) and meritocracy (in the House of Lords) gives us a
resilient model that defends a nation against the exercise of arbitrary
power. As a nation, we should be very cautious about interfering
further with what Burke recognised as a great strength to British
political, civil and social life.[8]

---

[7] McCall Smith, *The Charming Quirks of Others*, p. 103.

[8] There is not the space here to explore the real differences between Christian-heritage and
Muslim-heritage understandings of power and governance, but it is work that needs to be
done, especially as there are misunderstandings each way. Often, Islamic theorists appear
to find legitimacy for the political order only in the Qur'an; in the theocratic conflation
of temporal and spiritual authority, which is very different to what I am describing here.
Norman also flags up the need for further work: 'The stage is thus set for possible conflict
between the British sovereign demand for obedience to civil authority, and the constitutive
requirement on traditional Muslims, including those in Britain, to obey the Sharia', *op. cit.*,
p. 159. But I know Muslims who do not see conflict between British law and Sharia law;
who argue that the requirement for Muslims is to live under the law of the land.

# To serve is perfect freedom

Burke believed that freedom in society came through the protection offered by its institutions against the arbitrary use of power by any one part. Those institutions carry forward the wisdom of the past, through the present and into the future. They are traditional, handed on from one generation to another. As this happens, a gradual evolution and reformation takes place, for 'A state', he said, 'without the means of some change is without the means of its conservation'.[9] Those who see the need for reform should look backwards as well as forwards:

> People will not look forward to posterity, who never look back to their ancestors. Besides, the people of England well know, that the idea of inheritance furnishes a sure principle of conservation and a sure principle of transmission; without at all excluding a principle of improvement.[10]

Gradual change, yes, but Burke did not like innovation. 'A spirit of innovation', he commented, 'is generally the result of a selfish temper and confined views'.[11] He distrusted the desire to begin again from scratch; the determination to turn over the old regimes, and bring in the new, rationalist, enlightened human world. He anticipated the utopian impulse which was to spur on the dreams of Marxist and Fascist alike. Instead, Burke called for a careful reformation of the parts of the system that did not work as well as they might, rather than a total overhaul. He was concerned that what was carried forward had an eye to past generations, the ancestors, whose wisdom had helped achieve the best of the present, and an eye to

---

[9] Burke, *Reflections*, p. 20.
[10] *Ibid.*, p. 31.
[11] *Ibid.*, p. 31.

future generations to whom those in the present had a sacred trust. Tradition, after all, means handing on, and in such a way the real freedom of people was preserved.

A traditional view of things means that the individual begins to see herself not as the prime identity, but as belonging to something much bigger than herself. She has a responsibility to receive, care for and hand on to the future something that is of worth. This might be a political system, or the fruits of an education, or the sense of values within a family.

> As the ends of such a partnership cannot be obtained in many generations, it becomes a partnership not only between those who are living, but between those who are living, those who are dead, and those who are to be born.[12]

The individual, in this account of things, belongs in society because society is more than the sum of the individual parts. You will see the same sense of tradition and continuity here, as Burke writes of the nation:

> A nation is not an idea only of local extent, and individual momentary aggregation; but it is an idea of continuity, which extends in time as well as in numbers and in space. And this is a choice not of one day, or one set of people, not a tumultuary and giddy choice; it is a deliberate election of ages and of generations; it is a constitution made by what is ten thousand times better than choice, it is made by the peculiar circumstances, occasions, tempers, dispositions, and moral, civil, and social habitudes of the people, which disclose themselves only in a long space of time. Nor is prescription of government formed upon blind, unmeaning

---

[12] *Ibid.*, p. 93.

prejudices – for man is a most unwise and most wise being. The individual is foolish; the multitude, for the moment, is foolish, when they act without deliberation; but the species is wise, and when time is given to it, as a species it always acts right.[13]

You could argue that Burke anticipated the direction that modernity (with its infatuation with the new, the utopian, the individual) would take, and was prescient in his commendation of tradition and continuity. What would it mean, in Western societies today, to take his words to heart? It would mean trusting not the foolishness of the individual but the traditional structures and patterns of life because they have stood the test of time, and are a positive way of protecting the freedoms of the members of society. It would be to look beyond the myth of modernity, and not always to indulge in wave after wave of new initiatives.

# The greatest and ancientest

## Who inspired Burke?

I hope something of the depth and wisdom of Burke comes through this all-too-brief review of his response to the French Revolution. He does have things to say that are challenging to the secular soul with its prejudices and assumptions, its excessive individualism, utilitarianism and narrow sense of 'identity'. His understanding of the relationship between the individual and society is different to the mainstream today, but has much to commend it. But his ideas did not come from nowhere.

---

[13] Cited by Russell Kirk, *The Conservative Mind: From Burke to Eliot*, Gateway Editions, Indianna, 6th revised edition, 1978, p. 50.

Kirk says that Burke inherited Richard Hooker with his Anglicanism; and Hooker looked back to the Schoolmen and their authorities.[14] Burke would often quote by heart these words from Hooker:

> The reason first why do we admire those things which are greatest, and second those things which are ancientest, is because the one are the least distant from the infinite substance, the other from the infinite continuance, of God.[15]

# No man is an island

We turn now to examine some of Burke's antecedents. We've mentioned John Donne already, writing at the beginning of the seventeenth century, as he reflects upon individuality.

> No man is an island entire of itself; every man is a piece of the continent, a part of the main; if a clod be washed away by the sea, Europe is the less, as well as if a promontory were, as well as any manner of thy friends or of thine own were; any man's death diminishes me, because I am involved in mankind. And therefore never send to know for whom the bell tolls; it tolls for thee.
>
> Any man's death diminishes me, because I am involved in mankind.

Donne wrote from his sickbed in 1624, as Dean of St Paul's Cathedral in London, having probably suffered from typhus, and heard the passing bell rung. Did it ring for him? Or for some other poor unfortunate? Donne is led to contemplate that his fate is inextricably tied up with that of his neighbour. If the bell tolls for his

---

14 Russell Kirk, *The Conservative Mind*, p. 6.
15 Russell Kirk, *Edmund Burke*, p. 210.

neighbour, it also tolls for him. If a clod is washed away by the sea, then the land is diminished. Donne, and his other contemporaries, worked within a social imaginary which was primarily corporate: they would have understood the word 'individual' to mean something very different to what it means today. His understanding was more etymologically accurate: 'that which is indivisible'. They would have found it inconceivable that the individual would assume, as in today's social imaginary, the place of an atomistic self, one of a number of clods.

## Lost in that crowd

We have already recognised that one of the real fears of the secular soul is that corporate belonging will mean that it will lose its individuality. It will become the same, conforming to the herd. The freedom of the modern individual is freedom from constraint, from having to tow the line; without freedom, there is the fear that the secular soul will sink beneath the mass of undifferentiated sameness. Troops and mass rallies saluting Hitler come to mind. 'Where would I be? Lost in that crowd? Unable to voice my dissent; crushed by a herd instinct?' Such fears are real, and understandable. But, I'd suggest, those fears should not blind us to what a good, healthy, corporate identity can look like.

Burke, Donne and Hooker would have known the epistles of St Paul. St Paul wrote this to the small church in Corinth which he founded soon after the death of Jesus Christ. It is a foundational text for Judaeo-Christian traditions of political thinking.

## The body is one and has many members

For just as the body is one and has many members, and all the members of the body, though many, are one body, so it is with

Christ. For in the one Spirit we were all baptised into one body – Jews or Greeks, slaves or free – and we were all made to drink of one Spirit.

Indeed, the body does not consist of one member but of many. If the foot were to say, 'Because I am not a hand, I do not belong to the body', that would not make it any less a part of the body. And if the ear were to say, 'Because I am not an eye, I do not belong to the body,' that would not make it any less a part of the body. If the whole body were an eye, where would the hearing be? If the whole body were hearing, where would the sense of smell be? But as it is, God arranged the members in the body, each one of them, as he chose. If all were a single member, where would the body be? As it is, there are many members, yet one body. The eye cannot say to the hand, 'I have no need of you', nor again the head to the feet, 'I have no need of you.' On the contrary, the members of the body that seem to be weaker are indispensable, and those members of the body that we think less honourable we clothe with greater honour, and our less respectable members are treated with greater respect; whereas our more respectable members do not need this. But God has so arranged the body, giving the greater honour to the inferior member, that there may be no dissension within the body, but the members may have the same care for one another. If one member suffers, all suffer together with it; if one member is honoured, all rejoice together with it. Now you are the body of Christ and individually members of it. (1 Cor., 12.12–27)

St Paul conceptualises the relationship between the member or individual, and the body or whole. What is subtle is that each member is different, and valued for its difference. 'If all were a single member, where would the body be?' If all were the same – if all were women, or gay, or old – then there would be no body, but a collective

would result, drawn together because they share an identity. I think
this distinction is difficult to grasp without a theological insight
here. What is the difference between a gang and a scout group?
One is collective, where true individuality is suppressed; the other
is corporate, where true individuality is celebrated. The corporate is
different to the collective. The word comes from the Latin, 'corpus',
which means 'body', and so we get 'corporation' and all the other
words that derive from it. The corporate was crucially important to
Burke as he advocated the 'little platoons' of civic association.

St Paul likens the community of the Church in Corinth to a body,
where each member or individual is an indivisible part of the whole.
No one part of the body can say to another 'I have no need of you' –
for just as you or I need our feet, or our hands, our eyes, or our guts,
so the social body needs all its members. 'Identity' does not matter,
either. All are welcome in this body, regardless of nationality or creed
– Jew or Greek, slave or free. Such 'identity' remains, for we are still
male or female, or black or white, but we become part of something
bigger. We drink of a Spirit that makes us one, while respecting our
individuality.

That's not all, though. St Paul took over this metaphor from
Roman law (and these antecedents would have been familiar to the
Corinthians who read his letter), where it was used by social philosophers to explain how the members of the body were subordinate
to the head. Paul says something very different. He argues that it
is the weaker and less honourable members of the body that are to
be treated with the greater honour for they are indispensable: 'our
less respectable members are treated with greater respect; whereas
our more respectable members do not need this'. How might this
translate from metaphor into reality? If you, for example, belong to a
swimming club, and there is a disabled member, then St Paul would
say that that person should get preferential treatment. In saying this

he is following what Jesus Christ taught, rather than what the ancient philosophers taught, for Christ welcomed tax collectors (universally hated) and sinners into his company before the rich and powerful. St Paul is following the lead of Christ, and turning the normal hierarchies of the world upside down. Kingship becomes service.

If we think of ourselves as belonging, first and foremost, to the body, as corporate rather than as individual, then our body, our society, will be one which sees all its members as indispensable, all needed. Moreover, the weaker ones, the ones we might be tempted to ignore or pass over, are actually the most important. The strong, by this account, should always be on the lookout for the weak and take care of their needs, thoughtfully and carefully. We belong together, whatever our abilities, failures, talents or gifts. We need to listen to each other, and attend to each other's needs, for each of us is required by the body. You may think that you can keep on walking, but if your feet are tired and grumbling, then you need to stop. And who knows which 'I' am? I may think I'm the head, but actually I'm a foot. A reminder not to allow myself to get too big for my boots.

When I see myself as a member of a body, then my individual rights become less important than my sense of responsibility to the body. Responsibility. What is it but the ability to respond, to listen, to react, even to allow others to take the initiative? I am responsible for my actions. If I am greedy, and destroy the trust of others, or if I am cruel, and make others fearful, then I need to answer to the body for my lack of care for the health of the body. I cannot go my own sweet way, especially if I intend to cause harm. The sinews of trust and virtue are crucial to the health of the body. Look at how the British banking system has been brought into disrepute by a culture of overpay, and the selfishness and greed of fat cats and unscrupulous financiers. The whole body, the whole society, has suffered as a result: a diminishing of trust among most, and poverty among those least able to bear it.

# Back behind the Enlightenment

This metaphor of society as a body, and the way St Paul used it, has had a powerful influence on Western traditions of political thinking, as we have seen with Edmund Burke. Paul includes in this passage the statement that the body, when it is constituted as Christ's body, has neither Jew nor Greek, slave nor free within it. He is saying that in Christ, no longer do former identities define us. In Christ we belong in a way that enables us to transcend tribal belonging and collective identity.

We are examining ideas here that take us back, behind the Enlightenment, and which draw upon the Christian heritage of political thought since the earliest days. This seems to fly in the face of received enlightenment, which would ask 'did anything good come out of the Dark Ages?'

# 6

# *The Enlightenment story*

Many people assume today that liberal egalitarianism began as the secular world took over from the religious world. How does the story go?

As we understand it now, in the twenty-first century, it goes like this. The Enlightenment began a process of secularisation because religion was inherently dangerous and violent. The modern era has done a tremendous service for peace, in taking the power out of religion. At the time of the Reformation, it became necessary to create nation states to protect religious people from each other. Cavanaugh argues that John Rawls and others take this line, and it is a simple story.

When the religious consensus of civil society was shattered by the Reformation, the passions excited by religion as such were loosed, and Catholics and the newly-minted Protestants began killing each other in the name of doctrinal loyalties. 'Transubstantiation, I say!' shouts the Catholic, jabbing his pike at the Lutheran heretic. 'Consubstantiation, damn you!' responds the Lutheran, firing a volley of lead at the papist deviant. The modern secular state and the privatisation of religion was necessary, therefore, to keep the peace among warring religious factions.[1]

Here's a nice summary of this prevailing orthodoxy:

Liberalism ... was born out of the cruelties of the religious civil wars, which forever rendered the claims of Christian charity a rebuke to all religious institutions and parties. If the faith was to survive at all, it would do so privately. The alternative then set, and still before us, is not one between classical virtue and liberal self-indulgence, but between cruel military and moral repression and violence, and a self-restraining tolerance that fences in the powerful to protect the freedom and safety of every citizen ...[2]

It really is worth pausing to question what is going on here, and listening to historians who see it very differently. David Bentley Hart is one. He has pointed out the delusions of this enlightened story:

The European wars of the sixteenth and seventeenth centuries ... inaugurated a new age of nationalist strife and state violence, prosecuted on a scale and with a degree of ferocity without any precedent in medieval history: wars of unification, revolutions, imperial adventures, colonialism, the rebirth of chattel slavery, endless irredentism, ideologically inspired frenzies of mass murder, nationalist cults, political terrorism, world wars – in short, the entire glorious record of European politics in the aftermath of a united Christendom. Far from the secular nation-state rescuing Western humanity from the chaos and butchery of sectarian strife, those wars were the birth

---

[1] William T. Cavanaugh, *Theopolitical Imagination*, London and New York, T&T Clark, 2002, p. 21.

[2] *Ibid.*, Cavanaugh cites Judith Shklar from her *Ordinary Vices* Cambridge, MA: Harvard University Press, 1984, p. 5.

pangs of the modern state and its limitless license to murder. And religious allegiances, anxieties, and hatred were used by regional princes merely as pretexts for conflicts whose causes, effects, and alliances had very little to do with faith or confessional loyalties.[3]

During this time 'religion' started to become a phenomenon, an identifiable thing, to be bracketed and observed. How 'religion' came be understood is a crucial part of the Enlightenment tale.

## Religion privatised and domesticated

Cavanaugh tells of the creation of the concept 'religion', whereby it came to mean 'a set of beliefs which is defined as personal conviction and which can exist separately from one's public loyalty to the state'. This process went hand in hand with the beginning of the state, and for Hobbes, Locke and Rousseau there is fundamental agreement among them that religion – the Church – needs to be domesticated in order to produce unity. We have seen how Rousseau did it. Locke also redefined 'religion' and relegated it to the private sphere of life, denying its social nature. Cavanaugh writes:

> Lockean liberalism can afford to be gracious toward 'religious pluralism' precisely because 'religion' as an interior matter is the state's own stepchild. Locke says that the state cannot coerce the religious conscience because of the irreducibly solitary nature of religious judgement; 'All the life and power of true religion consist in the inward and full persuasion of the mind.' But for the very same reason he categorically denies the social nature of the Church, which is redefined as a free association of like-minded individuals.[4]

---

[3] *Op. cit.*, p. 89. And it's also worth reading Peter Hitchens, Chapter 9: 'Are conflicts fought in the name of religion conflicts about religion?', *op. cit.*, p. 93.

[4] Cavanagh, *op. cit.*, p. 40.

Cavanaugh argues not that there have never been conflicts on the basis of religion, but rather that it is a myth that the secular state was developed in order to protect warring Christians from each other. Like Bentley Hart, he argues that we have understood it the wrong way around. Instead of the secular state keeping apart dangerous and violent religious fanatics, 'the dominance of the state over the Church in the sixteenth and seventeenth centuries allowed temporal rulers to direct doctrinal conflicts to secular ends. The new state required unchallenged authority within its borders, and so the domestication of the Church. Church leaders became acolytes of the state as the religion of the state replaced that of the Church.'[5]

Cavanaugh has described well the liberal account and defence of this particular relationship between secularism and religion, where religion is privatised and domesticated, and no longer undergirds the public sphere of society as a whole with its own conception of the corporate.

## Political theory in the Middle Ages

We need also to challenge the account that politics somehow began at the Enlightenment, with our friends, Hobbes, Locke and Rousseau. The truth is that there was a long history of political theory that stretched from St Paul (and behind him, into Roman law), through the history of the Mediaeval Church, which brought Western history to the point at which the Reformation happened and the Enlightenment was spawned. This political history was sophisticated, and dealt with exactly the issues we have been exploring: how is authority best exercised? How does society develop and reform? We have already noted, with Burke, the importance of the Magna Carta: this was not the only time when arbitrary, absolute power was challenged.

---

[5] *Ibid.*, p. 42.

In fact, one of the important roots of modern democracy can be traced back to the tussles of power within the Roman Catholic Church as it absorbed the principles of Roman law, and used them to develop a conciliar understanding of power, challenging the monarchical power of the Papacy. The conciliar movement of the 14th century did not propose 'one man, one vote', but leading thinkers did follow the principle that whatever affects all should be approved by all – in Latin: *ut quod omnes similiter tangit, ab omnibus comprobetur.* During the 14th century there was much political debate which laid the foundation for the Reformation and the beginning of the modern era. This debate happened within the Church.

That this history of political thinking is barely known today, outside Mediaeval history departments in universities, can be explained by that Enlightenment phenomenon we have already encountered: that the old, the traditional needs to be jettisoned to make way for the new, the innovatory. Instead, let us give credit where credit is due: the Church needs to be recognised as the primary corporate institution that over centuries developed a most sophisticated understanding of politics, stemming from its roots in St Paul's writings, and in the legacy of the ancient world, in classical writings that survived the fall of the Roman Empire in the fifth century. Our modern era was rooted in that thinking. Politics did not just begin with social contract theory.[6]

## The corporation

The development of the idea of the corporation was a key aspect of political theory that the modern world has inherited from the

---

[6] See Paul Avis, *Beyond the Reformation? Authority, Primacy and Unity in the Conciliar Tradition*, T&T Clark, London and New York, 2006 for more detail of this interesting history.

mediaeval world. Avis describes how corporate institutions within the Church, like the orders of friars, guilds and universities, developed.[7] He describes how, by about 1200, corporation theory began to be extended from particular groups within the Church to the whole Church as such, so that there was already fertile ground for the development of conciliar thinking:

> The thirteenth century saw the gradual extension and systematisation of the powers of members over against the head, until by the end of the century corporate representation by delegates who were given full powers to act was flourishing throughout western Europe.[8]

Political theorists, such as Nicholas of Cusa, came to see the community of the faithful as a source of authority as well as the papacy. Gradually, such thinking affected other institutions too, and theories of corporate power facilitated the development of late mediaeval cities and universities, guilds, associations and trusts.[9]

This era also saw the unravelling of the Church and 'secular' power as the nation states began to develop. The temporal and spiritual powers had long been distinguished from each other, and had tussled, particularly over who had the power to appoint bishops – the king or the pope. When the Papacy rejected the theories of Conciliarism, preferring to retain a monarchical model, it sought alliances with the royalty of Europe. Avis cites Anthony Black's comment that '[I]n preferring royalism to Conciliarism, the fifteenth century papacy contracted a

---

[7] An interesting case could be made for the roots of such corporate governance beginning life in the religious orders, and particularly with the Benedictine Rule. R.W. Southern tells the story of how the Benedictines brought stability and order, continuity and peace to a pre-civilised society in *Western Society and the Church in the Middle Ages*, Penguin, Harmondsworth, New York, 1970, pp. 233ff.

[8] Avis, *op. cit.*, p. 40.

[9] *Ibid.*, p. 102.

dangerous alliance'.[10] Before long, each nation state started to develop its own negotiation between crown and people, leaving the papacy high and dry, and religion ripe for privatisation.

The Reformation was not, then, a question of secular powers taking the ring to protect religious fanatics from each other, but rather the outworking of questions of political authority that had a long history, and which continued in different contexts and institutions through the seventeenth and eighteenth centuries, and on until our day.

## In England a distinctive path

In England a distinctive path was taken. The Elizabethan settlement of 1572 confirmed the reigning monarch as the Defender of the Faith.[11] She had power to choose bishops, but was crowned herself – to symbolise the divine source of her authority – by the Archbishop of Canterbury. During the seventeenth century, the impulses towards representative government developed, looking back to that first reformation, the Magna Carta, and to the political theory of the Conciliar movement. The struggle was continued: monarchy? Or some form of democracy? Theocracy, as the Divine Right of Kings? The seventeenth century saw one king executed, a protectorate, under Oliver Cromwell, and the restoration of the monarchy in 1662, an exiled king, and then, in 1688, constitutional monarchy. The Church of England became the established Church and as such has been a key formative influence on English culture. Richard Hooker, a foremost theologian and political thinker during the reign of Elizabeth I, had a direct and telling influence on Edmund Burke.

---

[10] Avis, *op. cit.*, p. 100.
[11] A title first conferred on Henry VIII by the Pope. The machinations of sixteenth century political and ecclesiastical history are captured in fiction by Hilary Mantel in her *Wolf Hall* and *Bring up the Bodies*, published 2009 and 2012, respectively by Fourth Estate, London.

I suggest that constitutional monarchy is the best way of expressing the Pauline teaching of the Body of Christ, representing, as it does, a head that serves the body. This idea is a sophisticated outworking of the ideas that were explored by the conciliar thinkers. The monarch has a prime position, but is bound by many kinds of checks and balances to the body which is parliament, made up of appointed (the House of Lords) and elected (the House of Commons) members chosen to serve the common good. In this way the ideals of the Conciliar Movement found an outlet in the relationship as it emerged between church and state in England. It is interesting to speculate whether, had the Roman Catholic Church not rejected the ideas of Conciliarism, the Reformation would have happened at all.

## The polity of the Church of England

When I was made Dean, I took an oath of allegiance to the Queen, and directed my words to the Lord Lieutenant, her representative in the county. I promised obedience, 'in all things lawful and honest', to the Bishop of the Diocese. And I promised also to abide by the statutes and constitution of the Cathedral, and to work collegially with the Chapter (some of whom are elected, others appointed), and the other bodies of governance at the Cathedral. My authority as Dean is checked and balanced by different sources of authority, representing the people, the Crown and the Church. Burke would approve. He would also see God behind each source of authority, working through the people, through the Crown, and through the Church to realise the best way for political governance to be exercised. This is a way of being the Church which refuses to be marginalised to the private sphere, but seeks to remain a benign influence in public life.

In parallel ways the Anglican Church and state have both developed as constitutional monarchies: the Church governs itself as an Episcopal and conciliar body.[12] And so we can see, I think, how Christian traditions of political thinking have a direct relevance on our political structures and systems today. The central question of how to check arbitrary power – whether theocratic or democratic – began in the Church, and, through the Anglican settlement, has had a profound influence on the development of the constitutional monarchy we enjoy in Britain today, and on how the Anglican Church governs itself throughout the world.

Burke argued within this tradition. His was a different understanding to the one which so often goes unquestioned in the liberal egalitarian mind. I suggest we do not dismiss too quickly, with the secular humanists, the role of religion in public life, but if we are unsure of God's existence, that we remain agnostic, for there are benefits to recognising a divine legitimacy to the way society is ordered, as a constitutional monarchy. It is a sense of loyalty to this tradition, and a belief that it is a good system that has proved its worth over centuries, that informs those who argue for the presence of Bishops in the House of Lords. The Establishment of the Church of England ensures that religion is not privatised, but offers another 'estate' to that of the Commons, the Lords, and the Crown, with its particular wisdom and perspective on what makes a good society.

## A pause to digest

We covered a lot of ground in the last section. Important ground. I hope I have established that the thought experiment that produced the Social Contract is not the only way to think about the individual

---

[12] In this way an ecclesiology emerged in England that was to follow Nicholas of Cusa who set a high value on councils, on synods at all levels of Church, so that decisions taken are informed by debate and discussion by all who will be affected by those decisions, and that decisions are not taken at a higher level than is necessary. See Avis, *op. cit.*, p. 103.

and society. When the Enlightenment thinkers and secular humanists today erase God from the political sphere, all that is left is 'the people' as a source of power. In Rousseau's hands we saw how absolute democracy became vulnerable to tyranny. Burke, on the other hand, belonged to a stream of political thinking that understood that divine, beneficent power flows through different authorities: the Crown, the aristocracy, the people and the Church. We have seen how the traditions of political thinking that Edmund Burke drew upon went back, via Hooker, beyond the Reformation to the conciliar movement, which in turn drew upon Roman law. Theology informed those political debates, and St Paul's passages on the Body of Christ in his letters had, and continue to have, a profound influence on how the individual is understood as a member of a body, unique and not subsumed into a collective herd.

I have argued that it is a real advantage not to hold to a fundamentalist atheism. If we find it difficult to assent to the existence of God, I would commend an honest agnosticism that allows the possibility of divine authority to continue as lifeblood for each in a triangulation of authority: monarch, meritocracy, people. It's resilient and, perhaps, as Burke could declare, it has the merits of being great and ancient. Hooker's rather good quotation again:

> The reason first why do we admire those things which are greatest, and second those things which are ancientest, is because the one are the least distant from the infinite substance, the other from the infinite continuance, of God.

If we do draw on theopolitical understandings of the corporate, with the individual members fully distinct, but not atomised clods, then the question becomes: How can corporate, associative belonging can be revitalised in British and Western society more generally today? Can we breathe life back life into the corporate; into the youth club, the school, the club, the association, the charity, the guild – indeed all times and places where people cohere to build something bigger than each? Burke wrote of the importance of little platoons of local association. For centuries the Church has supported and enhanced such groups, clubs and institutional life that sustain civil society. If the notion of the Big Society is going to gather momentum, then greater attention needs to be given to this crucial strand of political thinking. We shall return to this below.

# Part Three

# 7

# *The play of divine wisdom*

## A hard practical world

I have argued that British society owes a great deal to its Judaeo-Christian roots. In the last section we examined what those roots are within the political sphere. We traced back to the Middle Ages how questions of the nature of authority were tackled and how constitutional monarchy developed, and we focused on Edmund Burke's defence of corporate association and institutional life as a counter-point to the absolute democracy that became tyrannous during the French Revolution. I was concerned to show that the excessive individualism that many identify as a contemporary social evil had its roots in the romanticism of Rousseau, but that the resultant atomisation is not the only way that we can think about human nature. Edmund Burke came from a long line of Christian thinkers who looked back to St Paul to find that individuality is best realised in membership of social bodies.

In this section I focus on the second of the roots that British society has in its Judaeo-Christian heritage, by considering the aesthetic; or at least all that enables us to resist the worst excesses of a utilitarian and instrumental rationality.

We begin by playing a little, turning to a novel that illustrates a culture dominated by an instrumental rationality where the 'practical' is all.

## Oscar and Lucinda

Peter Carey's novel *Oscar and Lucinda* leads us to imagine what happens when gentle, rather odd characters make their way in New South Wales, in a hard land of different ghosts. Nothing from the old world can be taken for granted in the new Australian towns and bush. These nineteenth century Australian immigrants respond with a grand, futile, brittle gesture.

Oscar sets out for Australia as a missionary, leaving behind bigotry, poverty and class division. Lucinda, brought up in the colony of New South Wales, is orphaned young. She is a rich heiress and a rebel. She flees in the face of the behaviour expected of her. Both exhibit character traits that manifest internal confusion and rootlessness. Oscar gambles obsessively, Lucinda has a compulsive personality. They stand out from the crowd. Lucinda owns a glass works. Together they decide to build a church of glass and transport it by sea and over mountains to Boat Harbour, a small town. The journey will be perilous, but they are determined.

Carey extols the virtues of glass. He draws attention to Prince Rupert's drops, for example. Glass teardrops, formed by dropping molten glass into cold water. Resilient, the drop resists the hammer but shatters when its tail is broken. A thing of immense beauty, it is enhanced by its combination of fragility and strength. Like so many things of beauty, it can be shattered easily and turned to dust, ground glass, but when it is treasured, the fragile beauty of glass, it is of enduring and transparent worth.

Carey writes of England (Home). The Anglican Church at Home faces the shaking of the foundations caused by Darwin. The Christian religion, in the New World, is not rooted there. Lucinda 'could feel it in the still shadows along watercourses. She felt ghosts here, but not Christian ghosts, not John the Baptist or Jesus of Galilee. There were other spirits, other stories, slippery as shadows.'[1]

Back Home, Oscar's father, Theophilus Hopkins is a naturalist based in Devon and a member of the Plymouth Brethren. With a simple faith in the God who made the mysterious wonders of the natural world, Theophilus hates the Anglicans who are flawed and fallible. Oscar is given Christmas pudding by one of the servants and cannot understand his father's prohibition of it, as he is slapped for taking a mouthful. How can such a delicious taste be of the Devil? And so begins Oscar's journey into the Anglican Church. He finds an obsessive love of gambling (although he never gambles for self-gain) and, throughout, his faith is to him a wager.

What happens to faith when it is challenged by doubt? How does one continue to believe in God, in the face of the evidence of progressive, enlightened human reason? Peter Carey examines the widespread phenomenon, the loss of faith, through his two flawed characters, Oscar, now an Anglican clergyman, who goes to Sydney as a missionary, and Lucinda Leplastrier, who has bought a glass factory on the Darling Harbour. They met for supper and Oscar explains:

'Our whole faith is a wager, Miss Leplastrier. We bet – it is all in Pascal and very wise it is too, although the Queen of England might find him not nearly Presbyterian enough – we bet there is a God. We bet our life on it. We calculate the odds, the return, that

---

[1] Peter Carey, *Oscar and Lucinda*, University of Queensland Press, Queensland, p. 161.

we shall sit with the saints in paradise. Our anxiety about our bet will wake us before dawn in a cold sweat. We are out of bed and on our knees, even in the midst of winter. And God sees us, and sees us suffer. And how can this God, a God who sees us at prayer beside our bed ...' His hands were quite jerky in their movements. There was a wild sort of passion about him, and the eyes within that sharp-chinned face held the reflections of electric lamps. Lucinda felt the hair on the back of her neck stand up. Her eyelids came down. If she had been a cat she would have purred.

'I cannot see', he said, 'that such a God, whose fundamental requirement of us is that we gamble our mortal souls, every second of our temporal existence ... It is true! We must gamble every *instant* of our allotted span. We must stake *everything* on that unprovable fact of His existence.'[2]

Oscar and Lucinda stake everything on their plan to build a glass church and transport it into the bush, to the new town at Boat Harbour. It's a crazy idea.

'You could transport an entire cathedral and assemble it across the mountains. Can you imagine a glass cathedral?'

She could. She saw its steeples, domes, its flying buttresses, motes of dust, shafts of light. 'Mr Hopkins, we are mad to think of it.'

'Not mad, I pray not mad. But the sheer joy of contemplating it is hard to contain.'

She thought: I cannot separate love from glass; I must be just a little mad.

He said: 'I think it is this *feeling* that you are tempted to call madness, but there is a more accurate description ... but I will embarrass you ...'

---

[2] *Ibid.*, pp. 261–2.

'you need not protect me.'

'I embarrass myself. However ... it is ecstasy we are feeling.'[3]

And so the project is conceived. The church is built at Lucinda's glass factory. It is packed up and, extraordinarily, it survives the overland journey to Boat Harbour, where it is assembled and is floated into the town on the tide. Mr Percy Smith helps Oscar see how it will be possible:

> He stood up. He began to stride around the fire. 'Not then, now, here. On the barge. You see, I have worked it out. We will enter Boat Harbour in glory. Can you imagine it? Can you see the look on their godless faces? A crystal vision. My oh my. Can you see it, Mr Hopkins? What a visitation it would be to see God's temple come to them upon the water.' [4]

And so Oscar, the clergyman, sits inside the church as it floats up the river on two barges and enters the town. He sits inside the hot, brittle church, transparent to the world, with a prayer book on his knees. An Aboriginal woman, a Mary Magdalene figure, sees the sight, and becomes a Christian:

> When she saw this glass church she became a Christian. This was the day Jesus first came to the Bellinger. She saw Jesus, Mary, Joseph, Paul and Jonah – all that mob she never knew before. She saw [Oscar] was a brave man. She saw he had a halo like one of these saints.[5]

But, for Oscar, the wager (the hopes, the whole enterprise) is brittle. Inside the church, as he floats up the river on a makeshift

---

[3] *Ibid.*, pp. 391–2.
[4] *Ibid.*, p. 493.
[5] *Ibid.*, p. 496.

barge, it is hot, it is full of flies. The world of the naturalist calls the church into question: unimaginable, contradictory, impossible.

There were bush-flies inside the church. They did not understand glass walls. There were also three blue-bellied dragon-flies. For one hundred thousand years their progenitors had inhabited that valley without once encountering glass. Suddenly the air was hard where it should be soft. Likewise the tawny hard-shelled water beetle and the hang-legged wasp. They flew against the glass in panic. They had the wrong intelligence to grasp the nature of glass. They bashed against 'nothing' as if they were created only to demonstrate to Oscar Hopkins the limitations of his own understanding, his ignorance of God, and that the walls of hell itself might be made of something like this, unimaginable, contradictory, impossible.[6]

Glass, the brittle, the beautiful substance that so captures the imagination as it speaks of wonder, beauty and of God, is something that cannot be understood in the world of insects. The fly buzzes inside the bottle.

Lucinda and Oscar stake everything to defy the impulse to murder God by practical reasoning. Again and again we catch Lucinda thinking of various Australian settlers she meets: 'You dull man. You would murder God through the dullness of your imagination.'[7]

Peter Carey's novel reads like a lament. He grieves the loss of humanity which aspires to beauty and wonder and worships God, even if as a wager. And perhaps he means us to take glass to stand for all that is fragile about faith in the modern world. It is at the limit of human understanding: beyond its bounds thereof we must be silent.

---

[6] *Ibid.*, p. 502.
[7] *Ibid.*, p. 253.

# The irresistible power to destroy something so beautiful

Metaphors defy explanation. They can be pushed too far. Carey is delicate in his suggestion, for the reader is left to wonder and delight at his story telling, at his meaning. Prince Rupert's drops: you can watch them made and shattered, again and again on the internet – and somehow the reality is lost; the reality of holding one in your hand, holding the irresistible power to destroy something so beautiful.

Why is this here? Why I am writing about this parable on loss? I think because when we become so wrapped up in function, practicality, instrumental utility, we lose a great deal. And somehow, in my mind, the very uselessness of the Anglican Church offers something crucial to societies that become increasingly hard.

## A thing of beauty

I write as someone who is not unaware of its fallibility, but who considers the Anglican Church to be a thing of beauty. I hear Carey's lament for things of fragile beauty. The Anglican Church today is fragile, and its loss would be profound. But I know also that it continues to reshape and reform, with one eye to tradition, and another on the future. I trust it can find a renewed voice with which to speak on the meaning of life, of enduring qualities and virtues that enable people to be ends to each other, rather than means, reminding us to resist objectifying each other.

The Anglican Church can do this because it knows what it means to be fragile and vulnerable; it knows what it means to go wrong, and require forgiveness from those it has hurt in the past. A sense of tradition enables us to see that always good and ill are intertwined.

That far from it being the case that humanity is innately benign and good, its soul is profoundly ambivalent: a mixture of good and bad. Therefore utopian dreams, built upon the assumption of a good humanity, will never work. Because the human soul is capable of great goodness and great evil, always forgiveness is required. Loss is an inevitable part of the human condition; always loss has to be endured and that means suffering is an essential part of life. 'Suffering produces endurance, and endurance produces character, and character produces hope, and hope does not disappoint us', wrote St Paul to the Romans.

# Loss and failure

One of things that a religious sensibility offers is a way to deal with loss and failure, which is profoundly important in an age that can too often get caught up in utopian blueprints.

The Anglican Church has a chequered past and faces a very uncertain future. But it still witnesses a pattern of repentance for the past and the knowledge of forgiveness. It shows a way in which virtue can be reborn out of failure and repentance, and in which discipline helps to school us in self-control and patience. It offers an understanding of the human soul that has more to commend it, as a way of being a person in the twenty-first century, than the cardboard 'identities' that people so often present to the world.

*How was it, she wondered, that character could reveal itself so clearly in the structure of human flesh and bone? Jamie looked kind, and intelligent, and gentle, and that was what he was. Could it be otherwise? Could the faces of the wicked look like this, have this light behind them? Perhaps there could be a book of photographs*

*exploring face and character. Goebbels and Mussolini – they could
be there to illustrate the proposition at the beginning; Goebbels with
his pinched, rat-like features; Mussolini with his thuggish bully's face;
both perfect illustrations of the proposition that character shines
through. And from the other end of the spectrum? She wondered
about that. Nelson Mandela, perhaps, would be a good candidate;
his face was suffused with kindness, with a sort of joy that was
unmistakable; or Mother Teresa of Calcutta, whose lined, careworn
features were so transformed when she smiled. She could look severe,
sometimes, but that was the effect of suffering and the day-to-day
toll of caring for those for whom nobody else would care. And then
there were the politicians, some of whom so neatly illustrated pride,
ambition and cunning; the various types of bullies; soldiers whose
faces often seemed trained into hard, wooden expressions; sleek
bankers to remind us of the face of human greed; gentle doctors ... It
would be a book of clichés, she decided, demonstrating that stereotypes – for all that they be derided – are so often true. The eye is the
window to the soul. Of course it was.*[8]

A liberal egalitarian society, with its belief in utopian blueprints,
and progress, can be very unforgiving of failure. It can find it
extremely difficult to cope with loss. The loss of ideals, the loss of
vision, the loss of the dream. As a result, paradoxically, our society
becomes very conscious of loss.

## The loss of loss

In *Gentle Regrets*, Roger Scruton describes how he regained his
religion, and writes movingly about loss. He concludes the book
with his reflections on the *Jubilate Deo*. 'Once we came before God's

---

[8] McCall Smith, *The Charming Quirks of Others*, p. 73.

presence with a song; now we come before his absence with a sigh', he laments. What might it be like to lose religion, to lose what the Church of England brings to national life? Scruton writes, and I quote him at length from his final chapter 'Regaining my Religion':

> If you see things in that way you will find it difficult to share the view of Enlightenment thinkers that religious decline is no more than the loss of false beliefs; still less will you be able to accept the postmodernist vision of the world now liberated from absolutes, in which each of us constructs guidelines of his own, and that the only agreement that counts is the agreement to differ. The decline of Christianity, I maintain, involves, for many people, not the freedom from religious need, but the loss of concepts that would enable them to assuage it and, by assuaging it, to open their knowledge and their will to the human reality. For them the loss of religion is an epistemological loss – a loss of knowledge. Losing that knowledge is not a liberation but a fall.
>
> In our civilisation, therefore, religion is the force that has enabled us to bear our losses and so to face them as truly ours. The loss of religion makes real loss difficult to bear; hence people begin to flee from loss, to make light of it, or to expel from themselves the feelings that make it inevitable. ... Modern people pursue not penitence but pleasure, in the hope of achieving a condition in which renunciation is pointless since there is nothing to renounce. Renunciation of love is possible only when you have learned to love. This is why we see emerging a kind of contagious hardness of heart, an assumption on every side that there is no tragedy, no grief, no mourning, for there is nothing to mourn. There is neither love nor happiness – only fun. For us, one might be tempted to suggest, the loss of religion is the loss of loss ... Except that the loss need not occur.

Perhaps there is no more direct challenge to secular ways of thinking than the famous Hundredth Psalm, the *Jubilate Deo*, as translated in the BCP [Book of Common Prayer].

Once we have made the decision to turn back to the ways of duty, gratitude will flow naturally into us, and – so the psalmist reminds us – gratitude is the precondition of joy. Only those who give thanks are able to rejoice, for only they are conscious that life, freedom and wellbeing are not rights but gifts.

A gift is a reminder that others care for us. The doctrine of human rights is prompting us to forget that truth. And that is why it is leading to a world without joy. For if the good things of life are mine by right, why should I be grateful for receiving them?

Where there is no gratitude there is no love. Conversely, a world in which there is love is a world in which the good things of life are seen as privileges, not rights. It is a world where you are aware of the good will of others, and where you respond to that good will with a reciprocal bounty, giving what is in your power to give, even if it is only praise.[9]

# A world without joy?

From these reflections one receives the impression of a philosopher who, from no great church background as he grew up, has come to know the value to society of religion. His latest book, *The Face of God*, continues his question of what we lose when we efface God from the human condition.[10] Christianity bears the moral and emotional knowledge of a living tradition, in literature, music and art. It takes time to acquire, just as it takes time to be 'cultivated', but it does give

---

[9]  Scruton, *Gentle Regrets*, pp. 225–239 passim.

[10]  Scruton, *The Face of God, op. cit.*

the person the means to reflect and live well in contemporary society, and even contribute to that tradition in turn.

Religion promotes art and culture in this 'high' sense. Many churches hold such living traditions of art, music and literature, which feed the moral and emotional knowledge of society. The Book of Common Prayer and the King James Bible have given, over the centuries, a common language and idiom that have helped to form a national sense of character. When one has the *Jubilate Deo* off by heart, such words form us by their beauty and wisdom. In recent generations we have lost the habit of learning poetry, the Bible, prayers off by heart, and many are coming to see this as a loss. It was the *Jubilate Deo* that captured Scruton's imagination as he returned to his local rural church: words half-remembered from his childhood, recalling him to the praise of God whose love passes human understanding and who enables us to feel gratitude for gifts where nothing is required of in return. For a gift is not a contract.

O be joyful in the Lord, all ye lands: serve the Lord with gladness, and come before his presence with a song.

Be ye sure that the Lord he is God: it is he that hath made us and not we ourselves; we are his people and the sheep of his pasture.

O go your way into his gates with thanksgiving, and into his courts with praise: be thankful unto him, and speak good of his Name.

For the Lord he is gracious, his mercy is everlasting: and his truth endureth from generation to generation.

Religion provides the strength to endure the loss of success, life, community, even the loss of purpose. It does so by offering the knowledge of a deeper meaning that turns sadness to joy, shows how suffering and pain can be borne and even transformed. Without this knowledge, we can become seduced by success and utopian dreams, hooked by brittle goals and desires which do not ultimately satisfy.

Oscar commented:

> 'It is a dangerous word,' he said, smiling, entranced by her upper lip.
>
> 'Which word is that?'
>
> 'Practical. It is the word they use in Sydney when they wish to do something damaging to the spirit. Excuse me, you must think me rude.'
>
> 'No, no, although you must not hold *me* responsible for Sydney.'
>
> 'I never struck the term so much at Home. But here, you know, it is a word dull men use when they wish to hide the poverty of their imagination. But would you say it was "practical" to sing hymns, to give glory to God, to pray, to fast? And what is the practical purpose of a church? For if it is only to provide shelter for Christians – and my dear papa would take this view – then it is better to have your congregation gather in cobblers' rooms. But if your church, no matter how small, is also a celebration of God, then I would say I was the most practical man you have spoken to all year.' [11]

Oscar describes a new society that has lost its real end, which is to give glory to God. The secular soul is formed, often, by an instrumental rationality where 'practical' means are elevated over ends, because there is no real end to which we tend.[12]

John Hughes reminds us of that real end, in which human work and endeavour come to fruition. This is not a God of practical purpose and impoverished imagination, but is something rather different. Hughes draws on the mediaeval theologian and philosopher Thomas Aquinas as he tries to capture God's essence:

---

[11] Carey, *op cit.* p. 390.
[12] Scruton elaborates the relationship between the contingent and the necessary in Chapter 1 of *The Face of God, op. cit.*

God creates purely for the sake of the thing being created, gratui-
tously, out of sheer delight. He does not create out of any need or
lack in himself, nor instrumentally for any other purpose. God
works for no other rewards than his love for the thing made. God
creates without loss or exertion, without failure and with perfect
delight in the thing made. He simply says 'Let it be' and it is, and he
sees immediately that 'it was good.' God creates without alienation
because his 'thoughts' are themselves efficacious; his work cannot
fall short of his 'plan.' All the traditional polarities with which we
think of human labour are transcended here: God's work cannot
be opposed to thinking; ... God's work cannot be contrasted with
rest ... God's work cannot be contrasted with play, for its very
gratuity and immediate delight is precisely best understood as a
form of play. More fundamentally, God's work is somehow not
accidental to God; rather, he is what he does ...[13]

Worship of such a God puts our own work in perspective. It gives
it a real end and proper purpose because its meaning is found as
the best of what we offer contributes to God's creative work. As we
create we mirror the mind of the maker.[14] But also, crucially, when
we fail, we can be assured that something can be redeemed; joy can
be brought out of our sorrow and loss. There is an end that is greater
than us, in which our activity is always only a means. The ends we
achieve are only ever on the way to the real end which is with God
– is God. No work, however dirty, boring and routine, should be
demeaning of our humanity, because we are not slaves, but made in
the image of God, who delights in creation. George Herbert's poem
*The Elixir* seeks to capture this:

---

[13] John Hughes, *The End of Work: Theological Critiques of Capitalism*, Blackwell, Malden,
MA, Oxford, 2007, p. 266.
[14] See Dorothy L. Sayers, *The Mind of the Maker*, Continuum, London, 2002.

A servant with this clause
    Makes drudgery divine:
Who sweeps a room as for Thy laws,
    Makes that and th' action fine.

Without the knowledge of God as the ultimate end of human endeavour, our own efforts are always our own efforts, and always fall short. We become slaves to success and failure, in circumstances that become ever more demanding, and it is an enormous burden to bear. The secular soul works harder and harder, and forgets how to rest and play.

# 8

# *The best that the Anglican Church can give*

The secular soul needs, I believe, the best that the Church can give. Among other things this is a reminder that humanity belongs in a world that is not curtailed by ends set by the limits of human imagination. There are ends beyond ours. And those ends put our own ends, and means, in a different light. People and things become ends in themselves, and cannot be reduced to means that are merely servile. Here is the real dignity of humanity.

How we treat each other then finds its ethical frame. As St Paul says, there can be no law against such virtues as generosity, gentleness, patience, self-control, kindness, joy, love, peace or faithfulness. Society needs such a virtuous framework if it is to function properly. The world of work does not ultimately gain if it is a brutal place, where people are treated with impatience, inhumane expectations, even cruelty. If things go wrong, there should be a generosity of spirit and forgiveness, rather than condemnation. If performance is not up to scratch then people should be given the benefit of the doubt, and enabled to do better, in service of the organisation. There should be an expectation of high moral standards and integrity within society and a presumption of honesty. Such a moral framework is not coldly instrumental, but promotes a positive, humane environment, where the norm is virtuous interaction. Society needs religion to provide this generosity, this 'give' rather than 'take'.

Of course there is purpose, calculation and utility in life. Such things are essential. They are the means to all sorts of goods. It is simply when they become ends in themselves, because there is no sense of grace, or gift around, that the human spirit is reduced, and operates on a merely material plane, functioning with self-interest as the main motivation.

> *She did not say anything, but she knew exactly what he meant. To be able to imagine the other, and the experience of the other, was what wisdom was all about; but nobody talked about wisdom very much any more, nor virtue, perhaps because wisdom was not appreciated in a world of glitz and effect. We chose younger and younger politicians to lead us because they looked good on television and were sharp. But really we should be looking for wisdom, and choosing people who had acquired it; and such people, in general, looked bad on television – grey, lined, thoughtful.*[15]

# Man, that most complex being, is a very simple one in his eyes

## Bentham and utilitarianism

If Rousseau was the Enlightenment thinker who fathered the secular soul with his idea of the romantic individual contracting with other

---

[15] McCall Smith, *The Right Attitude to Rain*, p. 212.

individuals to form society, then Jeremy Bentham is one of its uncles. His utilitarianism is in focus here.

Bentham's slogan, 'the greatest good for the greatest number' is well known. He interpreted it to mean the greatest *happiness* for the greatest number, and, on the face of it, this seems a perfectly adequate dictum by which to live one's life. It has had a tremendous influence on the secular soul.

Perhaps the best way to find out more about Bentham is through the writing of J. S. Mill. Mill was born in 1806, and brought up by his father James, in close collaboration with Bentham. From them he received a focused and functional education. He was learning Greek by the age of three, he started arithmetic and Latin when he was eight, logic at 12, political economy when he was 13. Until he was 14, he saw no one of his own age, but mixed only with his father's utilitarian friends. He once said of himself, 'I never was a boy; never played at cricket; it was better to let Nature have her way'.[16] When he was 20, Mill fell into a deep depression. He emerged two years later, restored partly by the poetry of William Wordsworth. As a result, although he never totally discarded the utilitarianism he was brought up with, he become critical of Bentham in ways that are instructive for us.

In 1838 he wrote an essay on Bentham, and while he praised him for his reforming zeal, particularly of the feudal practices of the law, calling him 'the father of English innovation, both in doctrines and in institutions',[17] Mill was also highly critical of Bentham's narrowness of mind and lack of imagination. Mill rejected much of his mentor's position, with a passion born, perhaps, of a sense of lost childhood.

---

[16] Cited by Mary Warnock in John Stuart Mill, *Utilitarianism, Oh Liberty, Essay on Bentham*, edited with an introduction by Mary Warnock, Collins/Fontana, Glasgow, 1962, p. 10.

[17] *Ibid.*, p. 80.

His depiction of Bentham serves as a good characterisation of the sort of instrumental rationality that can beset our own culture and thinking; a reductionist, unimaginative, servile rationalism that does not admit the possibility of any knowledge, other than that which can be verified empirically. Bentham's lack of imagination meant that, according to Mill, he had no appreciation of poetry or beauty. '[His] knowledge of human nature is bounded. It is wholly empirical; and the empiricism of one who has had little experience'.[18]

Mill writes:

Man is conceived by Bentham as being susceptible of pleasures and pains, and governed in all his conduct partly by the different modifications of self-interest, and the passions commonly classed as selfish, partly by sympathies, or occasionally antipathies, towards other beings. And here Bentham's conception of human nature stops. He does not exclude religion; the prospect of divine rewards and punishments he includes under the head of 'self-regarding interest,' and the devotional feeling under that of sympathy with God. But the whole of the impelling or restraining principles, whether of this or of another world, which he recognizes, are either self-love, or love or hatred towards other sentient beings ...

Nor is it only the moral part of man's nature, in the strict sense of the term – the desire of perfection, or the feeling of an approving or of an accusing conscience – that he overlooks; he but faintly recognizes, as a fact in human nature, the pursuit of any other ideal end for its own sake. The sense of honour, and personal dignity – that feeling of personal exaltation and degradation which acts independently of other people's opinion, or even in defiance of it; the love of *beauty,* the passion of the artist; the love of *order,*

---

[18] *Ibid.*, p. 96.

of congruity, of consistency in all things, and conformity to their end; the love of *power*, not in the limited form of power over other human beings, but abstract power, the power of making our volitions effectual; the love of *action*, the thirst for movement and activity, a principle scarcely of less influence in human life than its opposite, the love of ease: – none of these powerful constituents of human nature are thought worthy of a place … Man, that most complex being, is a very simple one in his eyes. Even under the head of *sympathy*, his recognition does not extend to the more complex forms of the feeling – the love of *loving*, the need of a sympathizing support, or of objects of admiration or reverence.[19]

'Man, that most complex being, is a very simple one in his eyes'. This is a chilling account of what humanity is. You can feel Mill's exasperation and sense of loss for all that is loving and beautiful and exalted.

The influence of Benthamite utility runs deeply in British culture, despite the fierce rejection of it by people such as John Ruskin and William Morris in the 19th century, and poets throughout the decades. Bentham's utilitarian approach contributes to the formation of a secular soul, fuelling a mindset which has become dominant, and which, when it holds sway, reduces humanity to subhuman ways of thinking and behaving.

Bentham talked much of happiness. His slogan 'the greatest happiness for the greatest number' is widely adopted by many today as a good rule of thumb for ethics. But, to be honest, it is a poor guide to right action. It very quickly becomes corrupted and distorts desire, leaving those who seek happiness with souls easily seduced by the worst excesses of material consumerism. You will only be happy

---

[19]  *Ibid.*, pp. 100–1, emphasis original.

if you buy this make-up; have this holiday; wear this gear; play this computer game; find the perfect partner.

## Happiness

There is a growing literature on 'happiness'. I am sceptical, not because I am against happiness (who could be?), but because I worry when it is seen as the sole motivation in life. Yet, when happiness is seen as the by-product of virtue, that sense of joy and contentment when you have done something good or helpful, then it has its place. Too often, as Norman points out, it is linked to hedonism, and he is critical of where this can lead:

> Layard is a follower of the English philosopher Jeremy Bentham, founder of utilitarianism, and with Bentham he believes that happiness is 'hedonic' or based on pleasure: it is a state of mind, and the goal of public policy is to maximise the pleasure experienced through this state of mind by the largest possible number of people.[20]

We've already explored the transition from worker to consumer, and how the consumer's pursuit of happiness leaves her vulnerable to aggressive marketing. Happiness, when it is reduced to hedonism and turned into the main goal in life, demeans humanity, much as Bentham's utilitarian ideas leave human beings little more than soulless automatons. Bentham's limited thinking does not conceive of a person who might grow in character and whose imagination might be inspired by poetry (which he despised). It provides no resources for someone to grow in self-control so that the appeals of hedonism are contained and other life-enhancing habits and patterns of life area develop instead.

---

[20] Norman, *op. cit.*, p. 121.

Bentham has left a legacy of unimaginative, utilitarian thinking that positively distorts the human person. It is a sad, subhuman world that he presents to us, one that contributes to the secular soul, and which needs to be resisted if humanity is to flourish.

## Pulling together some threads

*Oscar and Lucinda* gives us a parable about the brittleness of useless beauty, illustrating the fragility of belief in the modern world. We have listened to Scruton speaking of loss in different ways, and how important religion is to enable humanity to live with loss. He goes so far as to say that the loss of religion is the loss of loss, of that profound emotional and moral engagement without which human existence becomes shallow and vacuous, and life becomes joyless, lacking gift and generosity.

We have turned to J. S. Mill and Bentham, critical of Bentham's legacy, particularly, of a cold, utilitarian mindset. He talked of happiness as if that were the main goal of life, and we have noted how prevalent 'happiness' is, commended as an end in today's Western culture. Is it enough to be happy? Bentham, like Gradgrind, watches over the formation of the secular soul in which the principle is realised by 'the greatest happiness for the greatest number'. We have considered what happens when we lose sight of our end in a God who creates for sheer delight, so that the delight is lost from work, and we slave too hard in exhausting and degrading ways. The secular soul becomes ensnared in a hedonistic materialism and a futile and endless search for 'happiness'. It seeks that which always eludes, and is left in a fearful world, with deadly, negative gruel to feed its impoverished imagination.

The fear of nothingness, of death, of waste is terrifying and so we create purpose for ourselves. Setting goals and strategies, following processes, striving to reach, and prove that we have reached, measurable targets, we construct a useful life that blocks out fear. We measure ourselves by success, because then we know what failure is. Failure is easy to manage, for we work harder and we make sure we succeed next time. It is a pattern very familiar in today's society.

We are shaped by a utilitarian, instrumental rationality that enables us to avoid the fear of nothingness. It functions very effectively to close down any deeper questions of ultimate meaning or end. If we do not see that we have any end, beyond that which we create for ourselves, then the purposes we create for ourselves become all-important. We claim, loudly, that all is contingent; that there is no ultimate meaning or end. But we are haunted, I would suggest, by the fear that we might be missing something. Perhaps, like Scruton, we come before the absence of God with a sigh.

Scruton found himself attending his local parish church one Sunday for evensong. We have seen already how the words of the *Jubilate Deo* opened his mind and prompted further reflection on the nature of gift, and the human response of gratitude. In the next section I follow this thought and explore a little what worship can offer in a world where the fear of death and failure can be so dominant. What might it be like to think of fear as a positive emotion that leads the soul towards ultimate questions and even the presence of God?

## The fear of the Lord is the beginning of wisdom

This section offers a somewhat deeper analysis of what can happen when someone comes to worship, suggesting that the liturgy of the Church enables participants to find a touchstone in their lives of enduring meaning. There can be – should be – a gravity and ultimacy that makes worship qualitatively different to any other human activity. I hope I can convey something of how crucial I believe this to be. Too often in Anglican churches a squeamish informality sets the tone of worship, instead of the sense of awe that should accompany the approach to the Godhead. Interestingly, Patrick Gale has one of his characters reflect on the Anglican Church today:

> Then there was its air of cheerful community clutter, which to his way of thinking typified the bit of this, bit of that compromise that was at the heart of all that was misguided in twenty-first-century Anglicanism, the lack of rigour that would surely prove its undoing.[21]

Anglicans need, perhaps, to be reminded of the psalmist, who says that it is the fear of the Lord that is the beginning of wisdom (Psalm 111). This is not a cosy, compromised, muddled and domesticated faith, but one inspired by the fear of the Lord. The fear of the Lord. Not the fear of failure, or any other one of innumerable fears that can take hold upon the secular soul.

It happens sometimes. We reach the end of the tether of our self-construction and are exhausted by fear. Sometimes we find ourselves turning to the Lord. But when we do, it's a very different sort of fear that we encounter. Or so Peter Hitchens found.

> No doubt I should be ashamed to confess that fear played a part in my return to religion. I could easily make up some other, more creditable story. But I should be even more ashamed to pretend that it did not. I have felt proper fear, not very often but enough to know that it is an important gift which helps us to think clearly at moments of danger ...
>
> But the most important time was when I stood in front of Rogier van der Weyden's great altarpiece, and trembled for the

---

[21] Gale, *op. cit.*, p. 332.

things of which my conscience was afraid (and is afraid). Fear is good for us, and helps us to escape from great dangers. Those who do not feel it are in permanent peril because they cannot see the risks that lie at their feet.

I went away chastened, and the effect has not worn off in nearly three decades. I have been back to look at it since, and it remains a great and powerful work. But it cannot do the same thing to me twice. I am no longer shocked by the realisation that I may be judged, since it has ever since then been obvious to me. And once again I have concluded that embarrassment was much the lesser of the two evils I faced.

I do not think I acted immediately on this discovery. But a year or so later I faced a private moral dilemma in which fear of doing an evil thing held me back from doing it, for which I remain immeasurably glad. Without Rogier van der Weyden, I might have done that thing.[22]

The fear of the Lord is the beginning of wisdom. Christians often try to explain it away, dumb it down. For how could a God of love expect fear of us? Respect, perhaps? But no, it is not just respect, it is fear. The fear of judgement. Hitchens experienced it, and each time one worships there should be a sense of deep seriousness. For it is here that the human being is face to face with his end; prompting the conscience to examine whether life has been lived as it should have been, loving God and loving neighbour without self-interest, greed or exploitation of others, but with kindness, and forgiveness, and a proper sense of the ultimate value of the life of others.

*Social embarrassment was like that: the memory of some faux pas or gaucherie, of some bit of bad behaviour on our part, brings a*

---

*sinking feeling later, makes us think,* was that really us? Did we do that?

*The words came back to her from the general confession of the Book of Common Prayer, on the subject of sins and transgressions:* The memory of them is grievous unto us. Yes, it was. The memory of them is grievous unto us.[23]

Perhaps more often than we realise we carry experiences that are grievous, heavy and burdensome. Times we have been cruel and humiliated others, when we have taken more than we deserve, materially or emotionally; or played the victim instead of taking responsibility. Such experiences are difficult to know what to do with and can continue to rankle. Guilt, fear for the state of your soul, shame: there is no real way out of such discomfort. The memory and grief remain. We face the question: is this really the sort of person I am?

Worship can bring a person face to face with the awfulness of such a question, and find it is not the end. Instead of endless escape away into purposeful activity, we find something altogether different, a deeper meaning that shapes experience. I am going to draw now on Romano Guardini, a Roman Catholic theologian from the early 20th century who wrote of the profundity of the liturgy. He brings together complex, seemingly disparate, themes – such as fear and play – as he commends the essential purposelessness, and profound meaning, of worship.

## To waste time for the sake of God

Romano Guardini wrote of abandoning the restlessness of purposeful activity that masks our fear.

---

[23] McCall Smith, *The Forgotten Affairs of Youth*, p. 99, emphasis original.

It is in this very aspect of the liturgy that its didactic aim is to be found, that of teaching the soul not to see purposes everywhere, not to be conscious of the end it wishes to attain, not to be desirous of being over clever and grown-up, but to understand simplicity in life. The soul must learn to abandon, at least in prayer, the restlessness of purposeful activity; it must learn to waste time for the sake of God, and to be prepared for the sacred game with sayings and thoughts and gestures, without always immediately asking "why?" and "wherefore?" It must learn not to be continually yearning to do something, to attack something, to accomplish something useful, but to play the divinely ordained game of the liturgy in liberty and beauty and holy joy before God.[24]

Herbert McCabe OP has said something very similar: that prayer is about wasting time in God.[25] Both are encouraging us to challenge the need to be useful and instrumental all the time.

Fear can bring us to the Lord. And then, as Guardini understands it, the fear of the Lord seems to encourage us to play.

## Lost in play

The art of play. It was Donald Winnicott who wrote so powerfully of the importance of play in a child's life.[26] In order for children to develop as

---

[24] Romano Guardini, *The Spirit of the Liturgy*, New York, The Crossroad Publishing Company, trans. Ada Lane, 1997. (First published in German in 1918 and in English in 1930.)
[25] See Herbert McCabe, OP, *God Still Matters*, Continuum, London and New York, 2002, p. 75, where he says 'But the very heart of prayer is not getting anything done. It is a waste of time, an even greater waste of time than play ... For a real absolute waste of time you have to go to prayer ... It is an absolute waste of time ... It is a sharing into the waste of time which is the interior life of the Godhead. God is not in himself productive or creative ... He is love, and his life is not like the life of the worker or artist but of lovers wasting time with each other uselessly. It is into this worthless activity that we enter in prayer. This, in the end, is what makes sense of it.'
[26] Winnicott, *Playing and Reality*, op cit.

human beings and grow into adult life, they need to play, taking risks emotionally and physically and finding the resources to cope with danger. With adults, Winnicott argued, the playfulness continues in art and culture that enables us to explore the world in greater emotional and moral depth. Adults play when they go to a play, or paint, or delight in a glorious piece of embroidery, or read a Donne sonnet. We talk of a child becoming 'lost in play'. The adult too can become lost in play as she contemplates beauty and finds her mind wandering over some aspect of life, for then we touch truth. Or the truth touches us.

When people come to worship, people come in the belief that there is something more to life than raw utility. They come, simply, to be in the presence of God, to be encountered by the truth that is revealed, given. To waste time for the sake of God, says Guardini, is to play the sacred game with sayings and thoughts and gestures. The liturgy is full of sayings and thoughts and gestures, which are of profound significance – just as a small child, playing, is caught up in the meaning of the rules and actions of the game. The liturgy is holy play, done for its own sake, or rather, for God's sake.

I want to commend the traditions and institutional life of the Church as offering real resources to Western society today in these terms. Rather surprisingly, perhaps, I want to do that, regardless of whether we believe in God or not, for the play of worship enables many things that are lost if the only question is whether God exists or not. The practice of worship within the living traditions and customs of the Church is worthwhile and meaningful for the space and time it gives to explore in the same way that play enables child and adult to grow.

T. S. Eliot wrote these lines of the place Little Gidding:

If you came this way,
Taking any route, starting from anywhere,
At any time or at any season,

It would always be the same: you would have to put off
Sense and notion. You are not here to verify,
Instruct yourself, or inform curiosity
Or carry report. You are here to kneel
Where prayer has been valid. And prayer is more
Than an order of words, the conscious occupation
Of the praying mind, or the sound of the voice praying.

There is something very different about worship to anything else
that human beings do, and it can only be understood by experiencing
it. Of course, often belief follows practice, and I would not be
completely honest if I did not declare my hope that, as a result of
reading this book, you might take yourself along to your local church
and give it a serious go, long enough to understand something of
what it is about. Doubt looks different after a year or so of church-
going. And the question of the existence of God looks different too.

It is perhaps a strange suggestion. Why should you even contemplate church-going, especially if you have had a bad experience in the
past, or it means a considerable change in your weekly routine? What
on earth might persuade you? Why should you trust Christianity and
its message enough to experience its practices for any length of time? I
hope to persuade you that there are real benefits to church-going; that
the traditions of Christianity can enrich our lives and enhance what
it means to be a human being in today's world. Faith is not the same
as certainty; it does not have all the answers. It offers fruits in life that
are not immediately obvious. It does require us to be open – with all
our doubts – to some of the deeper questions and to some of the most
profound art and music, allowing the aesthetic to move us and prompt
us to wonder if there is more to life than we previously thought. We
may think of ourselves, to begin with, as free to choose (to go or
not to go), but beginning to belong as a participant rather than as

an onlooker can have its effect. Some find themselves surprised by something rather bigger and more wonderful than they assumed, with imaginations caught up into a different wisdom. Religion has rewards that are difficult to see from the outside. And, of course, if after a proper length of time, church-going is not for you, at least you might have a better understanding, from the inside, of what motivates people to go, week in and week out. Perhaps, if it has always seemed rather a strange thing to do, it will not seem so irrational after all.

Let me try to capture something of what happens when I worship.

I come face to face with that love which is, paradoxically, more to be feared than anything else that can be imagined. I enter a realm that is not human, curtailed by petty purposes and mundane routines, but a realm of God – of delight, of holy joy, that transforms me and reminds me that my soul find its rest in God's eternal glory. Each time I enter the realm of worship, I face a moment of judgement that anticipates my final calling to account. To use biblical imagery I am naked before God, stripped and pruned, heated and refined, distilled and purified. The sins I recognise are taken out of my hands, and I find myself aware of what I have not begun to comprehend. I face the Lord in fear, and find my true meaning.

The liturgy holds those who worship through that encounter. Grace-filled liturgy brings knowledge of repentance and the assurance of forgiveness. It consoles and feeds with word and sacrament. It challenges us out of our narcissism and into service and love of neighbour. We encounter the real presence of Christ and we receive him in bread and wine.

# It is he that hath made us and not we ourselves

*A female grouse broke cover suddenly, cackling her alarm, running along the ground, head lowered, to avoid what she thought would*

*be her murderers. Isabel looked at her in pity, and felt a sudden
tenderness, brought on by love. Love paints the world, she thought,
enables us to see its beauty, its vulnerability, its preciousness. If we
are filled with love, we cannot hate, or destroy; there is no room for
such things.*[27]

It is a good counter-cultural thing to do, to worship. For it gives the
wherewithal to resist that insidious trend to make this colleague an
end to my means, to turn that situation to my advantage, regardless of
the cost to others, to be entrapped in materialistic hedonism. It makes
it possible to challenge the dehumanising utilitarianism around us.
It gives us eyes to look for wisdom, to value it, seeking to be wise
in our judgement, while knowing that our wisdom is not ours but
finds its source in the encounter with the truth of God experienced
in worship. In worship which begins in holy fear a different soul is
formed, a soul responsive to God, not entrapped by the narrow limits
of secularism.

## From the very first every type of rationalism has turned against it

There is a gracious spaciousness that is experienced wherever the
liturgy is offered to God, turning human minds and hearts away from
the brittle rationalities of the world, leading them to rest in eternity
if only for a brief span, before returning to the business of Monday.
Guardini expresses it thus:

> From the very first every type of rationalism has turned against it.
> The practice of the liturgy means that by the help of grace, under
> the guidance of the Church, we grow into living works of art before

---

[27] McCall Smith, *The Right Attitude to Rain*, p. 238.

God, with no other aim or purpose than that of living and existing in His sight; it means fulfilling God's Word and 'becoming as little children'; it means foregoing maturity with all its purposefulness, and confining oneself to play, as David did when he danced before the Ark. It may, of course, happen that those extremely clever people, who merely from being grown-up have lost all spiritual youth and spontaneity, will misunderstand this and jibe at it.

When we come for worship, we should not be driven by purpose and a sense of busyness, but rather taking the opportunity to enjoy the beauty of an excellent choral piece, or hold silence corporately, listening to the sounds that allow us to imagine the infinity of stars. Guardini is right, it seems to me, that the modern world, since the Enlightenment, has privileged a particular sort of purposeful rationality, which closes down the sense of mystery that allows people to see that which transcends the ordinary and makes it extraordinary, and others as ends in themselves, pointing only to God.

If Christianity is to be understood it needs to be experienced. And the most obvious way to experience Christianity is to participate in worship. The Anglican Church is part of the one, holy, Catholic Church and its liturgy has been passed on through the centuries, offering a tradition that has enriched, and continues to enrich our national culture in obvious and less obvious ways. That liturgy does a great many things, but mainly it enables people who attend to grow in moral habits of the heart that help them to fulfil the two great commandments of Jesus Christ: to love God, and to love their neighbour.

# 9

# *In whom we live and move and have our being*

## The one thing that only the Church does

Worship. It's an interesting word: etymologically linked with 'worth'.
It's what people offer to God that is worthy of God. Worship is the one
thing that only the Church does. Other religions don't tend to use the
word in quite the same way. There are many different styles within a
Church like the Anglican Church, across different cultures throughout
the world, charismatic, to evangelical, 'high' and 'low'. There are
different kinds of music and degrees of formality: all different ways
of 'playing', all reflecting differences of taste and preference, and
offering worship in which we feel at home or, conversely, in which
we do not. Despite the variety of form, the content should remain
recognisably Anglican, offering a common heritage that enables a
particular formation that reminds the individual that he belongs to
something greater and more enduring than himself. The liturgy does
not belong to humanity but to God. There is value in going even
when you do not feel like it, or when it is different to what you would

prefer. For then you are stretched out of yourself, challenged by the difference. Challenged, whatever the style, by the central message of Christianity, which is to live life in all its abundance. Challenged out of self-interest, and into the love of God, inspired to love your neighbour as yourself.

Worship takes and develops emotional and moral knowledge. It develops and sustains a positive outlook, where key qualities are emphasised: trust, kindness, gentleness, self-sacrifice. Of course, I am not saying that people who are not Christians cannot be these things. I am saying that church-going can help make them part of one's character and strengthen them in us. Many times I have not wanted to go. I have felt depressed or tired, out of sorts. Invariably, I have left worship better than I went, in a better frame of mind, with a sense of gratitude and grace. Having been given something, and feeling that I should give something in return to others. My soul grows as a result.

So, worship, like play, offers something to a brittle world. But it does mean that we need to get into the habit.

*They resumed their walk down the path. Jamie reached for his key. 'What if you know that you have to practise certain things? As musicians have to? We aren't born being able to play the piano.'*

*'That's precisely what I'm saying: in order to become better people, we must practise,' Isabel said.*[1]

## A strange ritual to the outsider

I commend here a different soul, a different understanding of human nature to that of the secular soul. I suggest that church worship enables us to develop as primarily corporate, not individual; to treat ourselves and others as ends in themselves, not in some utilitarian,

---

[1] McCall Smith, *The Lost Art of Gratitude*, p. 108.

instrumental way, as means to ends. I also hope to persuade that we fare better if we take 'character' instead of 'identity' as a key descriptive of what it means to be human. Each of these is supported and encouraged by regular church-going.

It can be a rather gloomy experience. Cole Moreton described it like this:

> They say that more people go shopping at IKEA on a Sunday than go to a church. Who can blame them? I would rather queue in flat-pack hell and eat reindeer balls than go back to St Gabriel and All Angels. I went there that day because it was nearest and because I do like an angel: it was (apparently) seeing one of them that got me into faith, years ago. I was late, of course. Only five minutes, but it was enough. They had started, so I thought, Fine, I'll just stay in the porch with the notices and the flowers, then I'll sneak in under cover of the music when they start a hymn. Only they didn't. The introduction went on for ages, until I either had to walk away or go in ... right in the middle of prayers. Some churches are welcoming. Some have comfortable chairs, subtle lighting and carpets in nice, warm tones. Not this one. My shoes slapped on stone and each step echoed as I made my way through the gloom towards the congregation, such as it was. One old man and two old ladies, sitting among pews that had once held a hundred, muttering 'Amen' with their eyes open. Up in the pulpit, looking down on all this emptiness and me, was Father Insipid. He smiled a watery smile. I smiled back and sat down. The pew creaked and the three fish-eyed septuagenarians turned slowly and stared.[2]

---

[2] Cole Moreton, *Is God Still an Englishman?* Little, Brown, London 2010, p. 5.

Rather bleak, isn't it?[3] That is certainly a risk you take, if you go along on spec. But not all churches are like this, by any means. Peter Hitchens describes how he rediscovered Christmas:

> I slipped into a carol service on a winter evening, diffident and anxious not to be seen. I knew perfectly well I was enjoying it, though I was unwilling to admit it. A few days later, I went to another one, this time with more confidence, and actually sang. I also knew perfectly well that I was losing my faith in politics and my trust in ambition, and urgently in need of something else on which to build the rest of my life.[4]

Church-going can seem a strange ritual to the outsider. What you will usually encounter, if you go along to an Anglican Church service on a Sunday morning, is the service called Holy Communion, or the Eucharist, or the Last Supper. These are all names for the same action, reflecting the different theological and traditional emphases that you will find in this broad church.

## Open hearts and minds

The service will be about an hour long, and, if it is Anglican, it usually follows a set pattern or process. Someone should greet you with a smile (even if you are late) and offer you an order of service.

As Moreton expected, there is usually a hymn near the beginning, before or after the minister or priest offers a traditional word of greeting that comes from the Bible. Everyone then joins in with a

---

[3] Though, in fact, I felt rather sorry for the 70-year-olds he encountered, and wondered if he'd seen them differently had one of them been his grandmother, and had struggled to get there, to church, this Sunday morning. Perhaps his failure to see their humanity is part of the problem (although, of course, I know he's writing for effect).

[4] Hitchens, *op. cit.*, p. 77.

prayer which asks for open hearts and minds, called the Collect for Purity.

The prayers of penitence follow. These are prayers that give the opportunity to say sorry, to repent of things that have been said or done that leave a sense of regret or remorse. And then the assurance of forgiveness, declared by the priest. Confession can be characterised in a way that trivialises it: Christians letting themselves off the hook – 'It's too easy. Do wrong, say sorry, receive forgiveness, do wrong again!' But actually there's something more profound going on, based on an understanding of human beings that accepts that we do wrong and go wrong, and, yes, we do wrong and go wrong again. Instead of resigning ourselves to that slippery slope, the Christian liturgy recognises that, at the same time, we might well have the motivation to change for the better, and that we need a new start to do so. However many times it takes.

Penitence is important. Forgiveness is central to Christianity and is key to understanding how the human person can grow and develop, morally and emotionally. I find it difficult to trust someone who cannot say sorry. It takes humility to do so.

*She looked heavenwards, and felt dizzied, as she always did when she looked up into an empty sky; the eye looked for something, some finite point to alight upon, and saw nothing. It might make one dizzy, she told herself, but it might make one humble, too. Our human pretensions, our sense that we were what mattered: all of this was put in its proper place by simply looking up at the sky and realising how very tiny and insignificant we were.* [5]

This part of the service enables participants to bring troubling stuff to God, in the company of others, and quietly recognise that we

---

[5] McCall Smith, *The Right Attitude to Rain*, p. 164.

are not perfect. That we are not the centre of the universe, whatever our narcissistic urges might suggest. This is the time to remember not only things we regret that we have done, or failed to do. It might also be the time to hold up times when through lack of confidence or anxiety, or despair, we have not lived life to the full. We have fallen short of what God requires of us. When we have closed down our imaginations and not welcomed new opportunities.

A society that cannot forgive is a brittle society. To be a member of a society is to take responsibility for one's life and, to do this, it is important to know how to forgive. And know how to ask to be forgiven. Because we all do things we regret, in thought, word and deed. Often we are not even aware of the hurt we have caused, but it is there all the same and it is still our responsibility.

Without room for forgiveness in society, other things take hold. Things such as pride, cruelty, resentment. In any society there will be people who need to be able to ask for forgiveness. People motivated by greed, who should feel shame when they take advantage of their good educations to turn things to their own advantage, to the cost of others. There will be those who treat others with contempt, who deliberately humiliate, who enjoy being cruel to the vulnerable. There will be people who are resentful, who think of themselves as hard-done-by, when their supposed rights have been infringed, or a sense of identity is felt to be under attack. Of course, there are people who *are* hard-done-by, and there are rights that *are* overlooked, and people *do* suffer unjust treatment. There *are* victims of abuse, and other people's greed. But when resentment is part of the fabric of society, the voices of the downtrodden are drowned out by the complaints of the habitually grievous fuelled by an inflated sense of entitlement.

# Devices and desires

The Church service reminds us of the devices and desires of our own hearts; the way in which we can deceive ourselves. I know when I have been full of resentment at times in my life. It has clouded my judgement, my self-perception. I have needed to be forgiven in order to be free to live life abundantly again.

> *Surely we should not worry too much about our uncharitable thoughts, as long as we did not act on them. And yet that was not the understanding that people had had in the past: did not the Book of Common Prayer say, 'I have sinned in thought, word and deed?' Or had we released ourselves from the tyranny of worrying about the things that the mind came up with? Isabel felt uncertain; the niggling doubt remained that perhaps there was something in purity of mind after all.*[6]

A sense of personal responsibility is essential here. It is very easy to duck that personal responsibility. To hide behind an 'identity' that enables you to blame everyone else. To repudiate the shame you know inside, and justify yourself with clever arguments. To allow contempt to dominate how you see others, judging them by the clothes they wear, how they speak, whether they have 'fish eyes'; to expect and see the worst. There is much to ask forgiveness for, when we come to this part of the service.

> *'No,' she said. 'But why don't you think about it now? Why don't you set yourself a penance? Penance comes in different forms – not just the mortification of the transgressor. It comes in doing something good for somebody else.' It was ancient language; people did not set*

---

[6] McCall Smith, *The Comfort of Saturdays*, p. 172.

*themselves penances any more. But did that mean that penance was no longer needed? Here, she thought, is a case which disproves that.*[7]

# A song of goodwill and the desire for peace

After confession, usually, the ancient words of the Gloria will be said or sung. The words echo what the shepherds heard in the fields, when the angels came to announce that Jesus was born in Bethlehem. Glory to God in the Highest, and peace to his people on earth. It is a song of goodwill, of desire for peace, of thankfulness.

It presents a picture of God who is lord and king, but not as the world understands lordship and kingship.

So often people think of God as a tyrant in the sky, dominant and demanding that we submit to his all powerful will. The language that traditionally is used of God can suggest that sort of a God. But actually, what is happening here is a reversal. Liturgically, the language calls into question the power structures of the world that are abusive and oppressive. At the heart of Christianity is a revelation of God who was in Jesus Christ, living life as a human being, dying a terrible death on the cross. This God is not powerful, like a tyrant, but powerful because God becomes human and shows a love that wins out, that is stronger than death.

Jesus' life reveals a God who is more interested in serving and loving one's neighbour than lording it over others. Christianity offers a different way of holding and using power. Not God the tyrant, but God who loves and serves.

You could even say this is a God who is a king of service. Even the word 'service', when it is used of church services, reminds us that giving and loving as service to God is the first step in learning to

---

[7] *Ibid.*, p. 220.

love others. At a service, we remind ourselves that loving and serving others is the most powerful thing we can do. It is the worthy offering that God wants of us. Serving God in worship reminds us to use power properly in our own lives, as a duty and responsibility to serve others in society, to build up the common life.[8]

## Of the saeculum

After the Gloria, the particular prayer of that Sunday is said. The Anglican Church follows a calendar that marks seasons through the year, all of which have different emphases expressed in colour, mood and tone. If it is Advent, the theme is waiting, expectancy (purple). Christmas is shot through with love (white, gold); Epiphany, with the surprise of gift (white, gold). Lent encourages us to reflect and be penitent (purple), leading to the sorrow of Good Friday (red). Easter brings us alive again with joy (white, gold). All the other days of the year fall in 'ordinary' time[9] are green, symbolising flourishing and growth. Saints (white, gold) and martyrs (red) are remembered through the year too.

In marking the seasons like this, the Church is offering something different to the secular world. (Even the word 'secular' betrays Christian roots: it originally meant 'of the saeculum', the age between the first coming of Christ and his return 'at the end of the age'. This original sense reminds us to think about time as in God's hands, not human ones.) Time and existence are meaningful, because there is a story, a narrative that shapes our lives. It is not the case of 'one damned thing after another' as history has been described, but an

---

[8] In this tradition, Queen Elizabeth II made her vow to serve the nation when she was made queen; a vow renewed on her Diamond Jubilee in February 2012.

[9] A word in general usage now that comes from the Christian heritage, meaning originally 'of the ordinal' or numbered as the Sundays are, after Trinity Sunday until Advent begins.

annual cycle that takes us through a rich and complex menu of emotion, which can help us to become more self-aware as we seek to understand more deeply how God is working his purpose out, as year succeeds to year. Following a calendar like this enables our souls to grow in emotional maturity.

It is a story that anyone can join, and it has had a profound impact on our art and culture, the story of suffering, death, and the love that triumphs over death. It is a story that worshippers re-enact each time they meet. It becomes familiar over time and enables the worshipper to seek healing, if need be, for wounds and scars that can be too deep for words. This is a safe environment, which becomes more safe as the individual starts to trust what is going on.[10] That does not happen immediately, of course. Sometimes it takes months, even years to begin to feel the full effect. It is important that what happens on a Sunday morning is repetitive, predictable. It may be strange to begin with, but the pattern holds firm.

The service takes worshippers on a journey. We have been greeted. We have opened our hearts and minds. We have said sorry. We have rejoiced at forgiveness. We have been reminded of the season, and we then listen to readings from the Bible, including, usually, a portion of the psalms.

## Ancient texts

These biblical readings are ancient texts that have stood the test of time. Usually they will be in contemporary English, translated from the ancient Greek and Hebrew. Sometimes they will be in the

---

[10]  Of course, instances come to mind of abusive, manipulative churches. They do exist. But they shouldn't, and the fact they do doesn't mean all churches are abusive and manipulative. Your run-of-the-mill Anglican church will be a safe, good place to be. If it isn't, you can always leave.

translation that was made in the early seventeenth century, called the King James Version, or the Authorised Version. This translation of the Bible into English has had an inestimable impact on the culture of Britain.[11]

The Bible readings will be followed by a sermon. Worshippers on the journey take time to reflect further on the Bible readings, on different aspects of life. Preaching is the opportunity to develop some theological insight or reflection in the light of current affairs, or local situations or issues. The sermon should be thought-provoking, intelligent and satisfying.

The sermon is followed by the Creed, which again, like the Gloria, is an ancient poem-like text that offers the skeleton of the Christian faith. The congregation says it together as a means of affirming their corporate faith. Often I have known individual members who have struggled with some part or another of the Creed. They can affirm some bits, but not others. The Virgin Birth, for example. Rather than walk away, or remain silent, or cross your fingers behind your back, such challenges are worth exploring further. Each part of the text was developed with intense scrutiny when it was first written in the era of the Early Church, and it is worth struggling with it as something given, a text that has stood the test of time. It has been said, almost unchanged, by generations before us, and will be said by generations to come. In reciting it together, the action itself reminds us that we belong to a communion of people not just gathered in the church on a particular occasion, but extending through time and space. The Creed offers an active symbol of continuity through time, and creates that continuity every time it is said. One's individuality, although important, finds its true place within a larger body of belief here.

---

[11] The year 2011 saw the 400-year centenary of that translation, and there were a number of books published that year to explore that impact further.

The Creed challenges you out of thinking that you know it all; into a wisdom that accepts that we do not understand everything. The Virgin Birth? Yes, a difficult thing to get your head around. But who knows? Perhaps it is one of those mysteries that it is worth simply living with, that enriches our lives precisely because we do not understand it.[12]

## It takes you out of yourself

Prayers of intercession follow. Intercession: the word means asking for someone or something to come between what will happen and what might happen. *In the power of the Spirit and union with Christ, let us pray to the Father.* We pray for others: for the world, for those who are sick or suffering, for those who are bereaved. Some, not all, Anglican churches pray for the souls of those who have died.

Who knows if prayer works? Perhaps asking if it 'works' or not is the wrong question. Certainly the least that can be said is that it takes you out of yourself. It makes you think about other people and their needs: whether in some distant part of the world where there is war, disaster or famine. Perhaps your neighbours sitting there, weeping because they have just lost a child. Prayer decentres us. It makes us move away from self, so we think about someone or something else. And in doing that, prayer helps us grow into a bigger self. It enhances in us a sense of moral proximity; care about our fellow human beings, however far or near. We attend with a particular focus on a person or situation, bringing the object of prayer to mind in special way.

And prayer is more common than we think. It is widespread. It does not just happen in church. Holding someone else in your

---

[12] Rowan Williams *Tokens of Trust: An Introduction to Christian Belief*, Canterbury Press, London, 2007, is a good place to take an understanding of Christianity further. The book is based upon the Creed.

thoughts, with or without the presence of God, is an action that makes us human. We express our compassion and love through prayer.[13] In Patrick Gale's novel, *A Perfectly Good Man*, the priest Barnaby Johnson describes to the coroner at the inquest how he prayed for a dying man.

> 'So, let me get this right for the record, Mr Johnson. Knowing Lenny Barnes to be dying, you did nothing to help him?'
>
> 'No. I helped him.'
>
> 'How?'
>
> 'By prayer. He asked me to pray for him. And I realized that was why he wanted me to be there at the end. For prayer. I administered Extreme Unction.'
>
> 'Could you explain?'
>
> 'I anointed him with chrism – holy oil – from this.' He held up his little oil bottle for her to see.
>
> 'You happened to have that with you although you didn't know his intentions?'
>
> 'I have it with me at all times, as I do my communion set. I never know when it might be needed. I am a priest, not a paramedic or a doctor. I have few skills. I've been on a first aid at work course – everyone on our parish team has – but I'm not confident that I could give CPR correctly. But I do know I can pray for a dying man's eternal soul and I am confident that prayer will offer comfort to the dying and will be heard with kindness by God.'[14]

---

[13] One of the most chilling accounts I've read recently of someone unable to empathise emerges from the pages of Julian Barnes' Man Booker prize winner 2011: *The Sense of an Ending*, Jonathan Cape, 2011. Tony Webster, who narrates the story, emerges as someone unable to have any emotional or moral imagination beyond his own impoverished perspective. His lack of self-awareness is told with brilliant insight. You can't imagine him praying.

[14] Gale, *op. cit.*, pp. 50–1.

# In whom our individuality assumes its wholeness

The congregation shares the peace. A moment of movement, of symbolising the words: *We are the Body of Christ. In the one Spirit we were all baptised into one Body. Let us then pursue all that makes for peace and builds up the common life.* Here is the corporate at the heart of Church life, where individuals know themselves to be indivisible.

A healthy church is made up of people of all generations: young and old. People of different backgrounds and cultures. Some wealthy, some not at all. All are reminded that they are equal at this point, equal through baptism in Christ in whom our individuality assumes its wholeness. St Paul writes on a number of occasions that in Christ there is no male or female, Jew or Greek, slave or free. This is the blueprint of equality. It does not matter what 'identity' we come with: in Christ the whole of humanity transcends its differences and becomes one. It is a vision of completeness, wholeness, that does not force unity, but which dreams of a peaceful, gentle time of peace when all will be one. Salvador Dali's picture of Christ on the cross captures the universality of the vision. And because each and every person is equal, throughout the world, imagined in God's presence, each is due equal attention regardless of circumstance or creed.

Throughout the service, there will be hymns and songs. The activity of singing together is powerful, and if the words have depth, and are worth knowing off by heart, which many Anglican hymns have, and are,[15] then they start to shape the person. I remember when I was nursing at Bethnal Green Hospital (then a 'geriatric' hospital) and giving an old lady a bedbath. She never had any visitors, and was suffering from some form of severe dementia. I remember singing a

---

[15] The Church of England owes an enormous debt to the Methodist Church for its hymnody.

well-known hymn, *The Lord's my Shepherd*, to the tune *Crimond*, and she joined in; the words remembered deeply inside her. She smiled for the first time since I had known her over the weeks I had cared for her. The familiarity of the words remembered was a gift, a moment of grace.

Gift is at the heart of the worship; a reminder that others love us. This is not a contractual way of being, where we have to earn love, brownie points for heaven, or we come thinking that we are owed the good things of life. Grace is essentially generous and joyous, but, like love, it cannot be demanded by right, or bargained with.

One of the hymns, sung at this point of the service, enables gifts to be brought forward. A sense of giftedness is crucial here, as worshippers are reminded that 'all things come from God, and of God's own do we give'. We receive everything in life as stewards, rather than as owners, and it is for us to act responsibly and charitably with what we have, remembering God's generosity of spirit. A verse from St John's gospel has it that 'God so loved the world that he gave his only Son, to the end that all that believe in him should not perish but have everlasting life'. Some people have described this as the Gospel in a sentence, and it does capture the way in which God can be understood as so loving, so generous, that he gives something exceptionally costly to the world, his own Son. Jesus Christ reveals God's nature as nothing or no one else can, uniquely, as he lived on earth, healing and teaching, forgiving and calling to account those who were greedy or high-bound by regulations and rules. Jesus Christ showed God's love as no other, and his birth, life and death are a revelation of God. Particularly his death, where he was prepared to die rather than give back vengeance for hatred, thereby breaking cycles of revenge by showing a love that forgives to the utmost. Jesus Christ died a dishonourable death – the lowest of the low, an outcast – because in doing so he showed that God's love is far more interested in freedom from death and hatred and the terrible negative things of existence than in protecting honour and pursuing vengeance. Resolving to follow his example of self-sacrifice, even to death, enables Christians to enjoy life knowing that they do not need to fear death, because love is stronger. John Donne's sonnet captures that refusal to fear death with a triumphant contempt that echoes St Paul who wrote Death, where is thy sting? Grave, where is thy victory?

Death be not proud, though some have called thee
Mighty and dreadfull, for, thou art not soe,
For, those, whom thou think'st, thou dost overthrow,
Die not, poore death, nor yet canst thou kill mee.
From rest and sleepe, which but thy pictures bee,
Much pleasure, then from thee, much more must flow,
And soonest our best men with thee doe goe,
Rest of their bones, and soules deliverie.
Thou art slave to Fate, Chance, kings, and desperate men,
And dost with poyson, warre, and sicknesse dwell,
And poppie, or charmes can make us sleepe as well,
And better then thy stroake; why swell'st thou then?
One short sleepe past, wee wake eternally,
And death shall be no more; death, thou shalt die.

The belief in life after death starts here, not with the desire for immortality, to live forever (for what could be worse?), but with a sense that God's love is so all-encompassing that nothing can separate us from that love, not even death. Life, both before and after death, becomes infinitely enriched as a result. The person living comes to see it as the gift of a love that transcends time and space.

Gift is at the heart of what comes next in the service, which is the Eucharistic prayer, said by the priest, but celebrated by the whole people of God. Not only those present, but also the communion of Saints, gather together for this sacrament, through all times and places.

## Do this in remembrance of me

The Eucharistic prayer recalls the Last Supper, when Jesus was with his disciples before he was betrayed by Judas, and handed over to the Roman authorities to be crucified. Jesus took bread and wine, and blessed them, and told his disciples to continue the practice, taking bread and wine, blessing them, breaking and sharing; eating and drinking them as his body and blood, remembering him.[16]

Some Christians believe that this ritual action is just that: a remembering of Jesus. Others believe that during this Eucharistic (which is Greek for thanksgiving) Prayer, the bread and wine on the altar really become the body and blood of Christ. That his Real Presence is there. It seems to me that this is right. I do not know how, and there have been many attempts to explain this, including complex philosophical theories, like transubstantiation, but nevertheless I believe we draw near to the truth which is love that passes our understanding at this point because Jesus Christ is really present in bread and wine.

If the Church believes that God was really present and lived in Jesus Christ then it is not so much more to believe, that Christ is

---

[16] St Paul illustrates how this became part of the practice of the Church from early days. See 1 Corinthians, Chapter 11, verses 23–6, where he wrote: 'For I received from the Lord what I also handed on to you, that the Lord Jesus on the night when he was betrayed took a loaf of bread, and when he had given thanks, he broke and said, "This is my body that is for you. Do this in remembrance of me." In the same way he took the cup also, after supper, saying, "This cup is the new covenant in my blood. Do this, as often as you drink it, in remembrance of me." For as often as you eat this bread and drink the cup, you proclaim the Lord's death until he comes.' The words from this text are used as part of the Eucharistic Prayer whenever it is said, a practice that has been continuous since the Early Church. The word 'tradition' comes from the Latin 'to hand on', so this is a very good example of a tradition in practice.

really present in bread and wine, showing God's nature most fully as a nature of love. Jesus lives on as the body of Christ, in the Church, and as the Church is fed with his Body and Blood.[17]

Do this in remembrance of me. It's an interesting word, 'remember'. If bodies have members, then we are re-membering Jesus Christ as we receive. Re-assembling the members of the body. We are re-membering all that is dismembered, both here and now, but also throughout the world. It is a key action of the Church, made possible not by human achievement, but because God's grace is there, within the Church, the real presence of Christ in the sacrament. God's active love creates the Body of Christ, which is also the Church, of which each individual is an indivisible part of the whole. The Church is remembered.

This action is absolutely central to the life of the Church. But not only of the Church. I would also claim that to be corporate in society relies upon this Real Presence of the Body of Christ. Our corporate nature as human beings takes its meaning and significance from the Eucharist, celebrated in Churches throughout the world. The Church mediates God's sacramental grace as the Body of Christ in the world.

## The sacrament of the Eucharist

It is not easy to write this. To assert that Christianity has anything to offer Western culture today flies in the face of received opinion. The secular soul tends to see Christianity as a dominant religion that has had its day, sinking with Britain's colonial past, a vestige of its former glory. Yes, it is good for the odd, occasional ceremony – a royal wedding, for instance, or a state funeral – but that is it, really.

---

[17] See Roger Scruton, *I Drink Therefore I Am: A Philosopher's Guide to Wine*, Continuum, London and New York, 2009, p. 169.

There is more to it than that, though. When I took the plunge and started to read theology, I certainly did not 'buy into' the Church and all it meant. I went happily along to Quaker meetings, and was as disparaging as the next person about the 'institutional' church and all its faults. Now, I think differently. I would argue that Christianity has offered an incredible amount to our political and social history. And perhaps the most important thing is the idea of the 'corporate', the body which draws its lifeblood from the sacrament of the Eucharist. Because of the reality of the Body of Christ, the Eucharist continues to feed humanity. Through the sacrament, God's grace sustains and challenges us to be human: human persons, and a human (and humane) society.

In so far as we turn our back on what Christianity offers and, as I argue, what the Anglican Church offers different societies around the world, we become ever more brittle.

## Concluding remarks

We have traced the way Bentham's utilitarian and instrumental philosophy has gripped the social imaginary of Britain and have wondered what is lost by such a mindset. We have dipped into Peter Carey's book *Oscar and Lucinda*, reading it as a parable of the loss of the Church of England in a hard, 'practical' world. We have heard Scruton's love for a religion that offers the knowledge and culture that enable people to experience life as a gift, rather than a right, and so experience joy. I have drawn on Romano Guardini's classic book *The Spirit of the Liturgy* to develop the idea that adults play when they come to worship, and such play allows us to experience our humanity in the range and depth of our emotional and moral response, as we are brought into the presence of God.

I commend the liturgy of the Anglican Church as a place where the secular soul can be inspired as the imagination is engaged with the profound meaning of life and death. That liturgy is one easily accessible place today where something different can be found to counter the pervasive utilitarianism of so much of Western society. Because worship is essentially useless and purposeless, at the most basic level it offers time to find the touchstone of one's life and strike the essential balance between reflection on and engagement with the world. For the believer what happens in worship is meaningful at whatever level one engages, for there is nothing coercive about worship: it should be grace-filled, joyful and transformative. The extraordinary thing about worship is that belief does so often follow practice. The regular attendance at church enables different horizons to come into view. It stretches one's imagination and the soul's response to God. Scruton argues in *The Face of God* that the scientific mind asks the wrong questions, so often hidebound as it is by a narrow rationalism that lacks the imagination to see that different subjects require different ways of knowing.[18] He says that it is when God is encountered as a relationship that God's presence becomes comprehensible.[19] It is at church worship that the encounter with the Real Presence of God in Christ occurs, and when it does, the soul grows in understanding in greater and greater depth things that before were beyond the horizon.[20]

At the end of the Eucharist the congregation will be told to '*Go in peace, to love and serve the Lord*', and members present will respond '*In the name of Christ. Amen*'. From worship, many Christians go out to do all sorts of voluntary work and acts of service, putting

---

18  Scruton, *op. cit.*, pp. 9ff.

19  *Ibid.*, p. 157.

20  *Ibid.*, p. 20.

into practice the injunction to love one's neighbour, strengthened and inspired by the meaning that their lives gain from worship. This double impulse, to love God and love neighbour, has given, and continues to give, a Judaeo-Christian foundation to Western society.

# Part Four

# 10

# *Character produces hope*

## Cardboard cut-out 'identity'

We have looked at two of our three Judaeo-Christian foundations to Western society. First, we have explored how the secular soul is marked by an excessive individualism that tends towards narcissism, making it vulnerable to shrewd markets that pander to its vanity. That individualistic soul also becomes the atomised element required by the Enlightenment notion of a social contract necessary for the modern democratic state. I have argued that Edmund Burke deserves greater attention for his advocacy of the corporate and institutional structures that enable society to sustain itself and hand on moral goods from one generation to another. We have also seen how Bentham's utilitarianism and pre-occupation with happiness has a strong grip on the secular soul, and how church worship provides a crucial place to rediscover a sense of meaning, and the encouragement to lead lives of public service and love of one's neighbour. Christianity has provided, and continues to provide, political and non-utilitarian influences to shape the human soul. From the political and the aesthetic, we turn now to the third, to the moral. I want to develop this theme by considering the prevalent way we have of understanding 'identity' in Western culture.

## A persistent default mindset

You will see a particular process that can happen to individuals when they have a sense of 'identity'. Such a person seems only to understand himself by reference to an 'other' (whoever the 'other' might be – parent, other gang, authority figure, dominant culture). They talk about 'me and my identity' and become shaped within an 'us and them' mentality. Then, too often, an enduring attitude develops that becomes a self-fulfilling prophecy. 'I'm hard done by; no one cares; society has let me down'. A persistent default mindset solidifies into a feeling of grievance and resentment: the young person, who feels the world owes her, never really grows up into an adult who can forgive, and live.

> *'So you often come across boys who are quite lost. They retreat into themselves or their cults. Skateboarders are an example of that. Or at least some of them are.'*
>
> *Isabel thought about skateboarders. It was not an attractive group, with their lack of interest in anything much except their repetitive twirls and gymnastic tricks. They tended to be teenagers though, and teenagers grew up, although sometimes one saw older skateboarders, almost into their thirties, over- grown boys stuck in the ways of youth. She shuddered. Certain groups of people made her shudder: extremists, with their ideologies of hate; the proud; the arrogant; the narcissistic socialites of celebrity culture. And yet all of these were* people, *and one should love people, or try to …*
>
> *'Skateboarders are typical of the refuge cult,' said Jillian. 'They retreat into the group and don't really talk to anybody else.'*

*Isabel said that she thought that many teenagers did that, and not just skateboarders. Yes, that was true, Jillian said, but skateboarders were an extreme example. 'They block out the rest of the world, you know. They think that there are skaters and then there are the rest. It's that bad.' She waited a moment, and then added: 'I know about this, you see. Our son became one. He didn't talk to us for two and a half years. Just a few grunts. That was all.'*

*'But he came back?'*

*'Yes. He came back. But he had wasted those precious years of youth. Think what he might have seen and done, instead of spending his time on streets, skating aimlessly. Just think.'*

*'We all have our ways of wasting time,' said Isabel. 'Think of golf ... What's your son doing now?'*

*'He works for a hedge fund.'*[21]

# 'Us and them'

The temptation to divide into 'us and them' groups is pervasive and perennial. People form into groups with like-minded others to find a sense of solidarity, often built around a grievance. The negative is projected away, all the ills of the world, onto the other, and becomes the fault of 'them'. A blame culture is born, and we are the resentful victims of the evils of others. There are many examples in literature, and you certainly see it in many of the stories of the Judaeo-Christian scriptures. It is what makes the story of the Good Samaritan such a powerful account, for here was someone who belonged to the supposedly 'victim' class helping out a Jewish person, where other Jewish people walked by on the other side of the road. The Samaritans

---

[21] McCall Smith, *The Charming Quirks of Others*, pp. 39–40.

were reviled and treated with contempt and, in the story, he was the
one who went out of his way to help. He was the one who showed
mercy.[22]

We have looked back into history to discover the philosophical
roots of the secular soul as it has become individualistic and utilitarian. We now do something similar, as we explore 'identity'.

## A history of 'us and them', beginning with Hegel

You could say that the phenomenon of 'us and them' was first described
philosophically by Hegel (1770–1831). In his *Phenomenology of the
Spirit* he explains what can happen, and he suggests that this is a
dynamic that occurs both within the human person, and in society
at large. It is both an internal phenomenon, and an external one.[23]

Hegel writes of two subjects, who are in conflict, because each only
knows who he is if he can do the other down. One wins out: Hegel
calls him the Master or the Lord. The other is the Bondsman or Slave.
The Master, because he is dominant, now can sit by and enjoy leisure,
because the Slave does everything for him.

That is not the end of the story, though. For the Slave, although
he is doing things that he does not chose and is therefore alienated
from what he produces, he is nevertheless working, creative and
productive, even if it is only in service. He develops as a person in
a way the Master does not. The Master, because he is idle, starts to
withdraw, in terms of his active engagement with what makes him a
person. The Slave becomes more of a person, and eventually overtakes
the Master, and their positions are reversed. Then, Hegel suggests, the
cycle begins again, for the Slave is now the new Master, and subjugates

---

[22] The gospel of St Luke, 10: 25–37.
[23] Hegel's *Phenomenology of Spirit*, part B, iv, A: 'Independence and Dependence of
Self-Consciousness: Lordship and Bondage.'

the old Master in turn. The cycle continues until both realise that their subjectivity does not need this dynamic: that 'I' do not need 'you' to fight against in order to be 'me'. We both can transcend the cycle, and find our subjectivity in a different sort of freedom.

This parable has had an enormous impact on philosophers since.[24] Let us look briefly at some key thinkers who have taken it up.

Karl Marx understood the Master/Slave dyad to be a basic struggle between the bourgeoisie and the proletariat, between the 'haves' and the 'have nots'. He thought that history proceeded with an ongoing war at the socio-economic level between these different classes. Reconciliation would come at the end of history, with the arrival of the classless society. Then capitalism would be overthrown, and none would be alienated from their labour.[25]

Nietzsche, too, used this basic division between Master and Slave, although he gave it a moral twist. The Slave has a herd mentality, and succumbs to a morality that slavishly obeys a degraded understanding of good and evil. Only the Master – or, as he called it, the Übermensch or Superman – rises above the conventional 'good and evil' onto a different plane, where the will to power can be exercised in freedom from the constraints of the herd. The Übermensch commands mastery of others by his will power, the result of a character of fortitude and excellence.

Nietzsche is a profoundly important philosopher, and it is worth pausing a moment or two to consider his impact further. He hated

---

[24] Although it's interesting to contrast it with the parable that Jesus taught, of the Good Samaritan, where the other (in society's terms, the disadvantaged, outcast) serves the vulnerable, but dominant in society's terms, rather than competing. Perhaps Hegel's myth is not the only place we need to start. Or again, perhaps Jesus' parable only makes sense against the normal expectation that people will seek to do the Other down.

[25] See John Hughes, *op. cit.*, for a really good discussion of the Marxist (and other) understanding of work.

Christianity for what he saw as its weakness. He believed it was a passive-aggressive religion in its manipulation of people in their needs, and largely responsible for creating the herd mentality of the Slave, encouraging people to become self-sacrificial doormats. He famously declared the death of God, albeit with a certain romantic wistfulness. Nietzsche foresaw a world without God, and advocated, in the place of God, human 'will-to-power'. In doing so, he harkened back to the heroic figure of ancient Greek philosophy, to the ideal of excellence found in the writings of Plato and Aristotle. Nietzsche thought Christianity was motivated by resentment, the resentment of the weak. In the place of Christianity and its snivelling weakness, he offered the heroic strength of the Superman, whose desires were of such an order that they would be worth repeating, eternally. The metaphysical idea of the eternal recurrence was Nietzsche's as he imagined the Superman, always willing the most excellent thing, to eternity. Heroic strength, though, not love.

He has been accused of nihilism, because without a religious world view, all that is left is the human will. Without some absolute that is beyond human existence, when God is dead, the world is left drained of meaning, apart from what humanity can construct for itself (and so he heavily influenced John Paul Sartre, and the Existentialist school of the twentieth century). Nietzsche discarded the conventional, religious understanding of good and evil bequeathed by Christianity, in favour of the Übermensch which creates its own heroic morality. But instead of a race of giants, humanity is left in a world where all is relative, without any moral referent outside itself, and which therefore, ultimately, lacks any moral seriousness or way to judge good from evil. Such a world is nihilistic, based on nothing, and becomes a living hell of human conflict, the struggle of opposing heroes as they rise above the herd to assert their will to power. David Bentley Hart argues that Nietzsche's instincts failed him; that he failed to see the audacious creativity that was – and is – at the heart of Christianity: 'a grand reimagining of the possibilities of human existence [which] would not have been possible had it not been sustained by a genuine and generous happiness'.[26]

> *Equality was dull, and goodness was dull, too, if one reflected on it; and Nietzsche, of course, would have agreed. Peace was dull; conflict and violence were exciting ... There was slavery still; debt bondage; enforced prostitution; trafficking in children. It was all there, but the voices that spoke about it were so hard to hear amongst all the trivia and noise and the profound loss of moral seriousness.[27]*

Michel Foucault was heavily influenced by Nietzsche, taking up the concept of the will to power. His analysis was that power is everywhere, in all human relations and institutions, and the Master is there, in dominant discourses that subjugate the subordinated by controlling knowledge and regulating behaviour to the extent that submission becomes internalised. With Foucault, the concept of 'power' becomes the lens through which all human experience is viewed.

Foucault has had a profound influence on the academic world of today. When I wrote my doctoral thesis in the late 1990s, he was the philosopher I used as the theorist of power to shape its argument. I would now write a very different PhD, using other tools of analysis and reaching very different conclusions. It is interesting to observe how I have changed my mind.

Looking back now it is clear that my thesis, like this book, expressed an enduring interest in corporate identity. Then I examined an inner city Church of England congregation, wondering what enabled it to cohere, given that its regular membership was drawn

---

[26] Hart, *op. cit.*, p. 174.
[27] McCall Smith, *Friends, Lovers, Chocolate*, p. 193.

from eleven different countries of origin. I used the traditional methods of ethnography (participant observation, guided interviews) and analysed what people told me about their experience of church-going. Many remembered the Windrush experience: the cold reception they had received from the Church of England in the 1950s (to its shame). Those who had stuck with the Church of England did so despite, I assumed, often not feeling at home.

I was particularly interested in how people who were different (to the norm of white and male) negotiated their place within the dominant discourse of Anglicanism, and how, when they did not feel that they were being heard, they would (unconsciously, on the whole) use other discursive practices, such as gossip, to give themselves a sense of solidarity, and to help them find a voice, if not within the structures of governance and authority, then outside them. I also explored how sickness and absence played their part in expressing non-participation. I argued that the corporate identity was sustained by the dominant Anglican liturgy and worship, but that many did not feel they belonged within it and they bore the cost of their alienation. It was a difficult thesis to write[28] and now I suspect I know why, over and above the usual difficulties of ethnographic research.

To use Michel Foucault in order to analyse the data I collected was to take for granted that relations of power permeate all institutional life. For Foucault such relations of power are binary – and this is where I would argue he belongs within the trajectory I am describing that began with Hegel. For Foucault, institutional practices shape life, and people either benefit, as dominant, or do not, as subordinate. Inevitably, then, class, gender and race are the markers of

---

[28] See my 'The Messiness of Studying Congregations' in Mathew Guest, Karin Tusting and Linda Woodhead (eds), *Congregational Studies in the UK: Christianity in a Post-Christian Context*, Ashgate, Aldershot and Burlington, VT, 2004, pp. 125–37.

subordination in a church community that was dominated by a white, middle-class, male-led Anglican ethos and culture and so the most subordinated would be the black, female and lower-class people. Now I am well aware that the Anglican Church can be, and has been, patrician, and that it has often lived up to its reputation of privilege and class. But looking back on it, I realise how blatantly I was bringing to my data a certain ideological mindset that did not do justice to what was really the case.

This congregation, and those who led it, actually worked extremely hard and effectively to enable people of very different backgrounds to feel at home. Its traditional means of incorporation, of creating a corporate identity, were sound and good. The worship was inclusive and friendly, yet strong enough to hold everyone who came because its repeated patterns allowed a sense of transcendence that took people out of the particularities of individual 'identity' and into something bigger. As they gathered to receive the sacrament of the Eucharist, they became the Body of Christ.

I failed, because of my adherence to Foucault, to appreciate that the corporate identity of this church community worked. And, ultimately, using those tools of analysis, I missed what it achieved. As I look back now, I know I did recognise the strong corporate life of the congregation, but I suppressed that voice within me, for the sake of the particular ideological mindset that I brought to the research which was, actually, a straitjacket. Moreover it turned black, female, working-class people into victims which they most certainly were not. I was seduced, I would say now, by a philosopher whose influence is pervasive through the corridors of Western intellectual life, except in France, where is he widely regarded as a charlatan.[29]

---

[29] Scruton, *Gentle Regrets*, p. 36. See also Chapter 11 in *Modern Culture* entitled 'Idle Hands' for a further critique of Michel Foucault.

# Cycles of resentment

The basic binary that I am describing has been profoundly influential on much thinking in academic circles and within society, resulting in a pervasive sense that there are two camps, the 'haves' and the 'have nots', the dominant and the subordinate. The discourse of 'identity' belongs here, I think, as it enables 'the subordinate' to reflect upon their lack of power. You see that basic binary at work in post-colonial studies, which looks to the cultural theorist Edward Said as a father figure. He wrote a book in 1978 entitled *Orientalism*, which described the relationship between the West and the East (particularly the Muslim world) in these binary terms. His thesis, and particularly his way of writing history, which borrowed much from Foucault's methods, has been largely discredited as factually and theoretically flawed, but he, and this way of thinking, continues to have a real influence.[30]

One of the consequences of *Orientalism* has been to fuel an ideological Islam with a sense of grievance against the West. That grievance becomes blind to what real historical grounds there are for bitterness towards the West, and fails to note the real advantages there have been to a strong cross-fertilisation between the occidental and oriental worlds. Instead there has been a hardening into extremist views for which Said has been a catalyst. Stirring a

---

[30] A number of books on Edward Said have critiqued his theories. See Robert Irwin, *For Lust of Knowing: The Orientalists and their Enemies*, Penguin Books, London, 2007; Ibn Warraq, *Defending the West: A Critique of Edward Said's Orientalism*, Prometheus Books, New York, 2007; Daniel Martin Varisco, *Reading Orientalism: Said and the Unsaid*, University of Washington Press, Seattle, WA. and London, 2007. Roger Scruton's *The West and the Rest: Globalization and the Terrorist Threat*, Continuum, London and New York, 2002, is also worth reading for its analysis of the Clash of civilisations theory developed by Samuel Huntingdon, which in turn draws somewhat from Edward Said's post-colonial theories.

legacy of guilt within the 'dominant' Western academic communities, such extremist views become more difficult to engage with honestly, with the aim to seek where the truth lies. The self-perceived Slave is resentful, in Hegel's terms, and the Master feels guilt. Both become trapped in this psychological exchange which has fear of the other at its heart. Without forgiveness, there is no creative reconciliation.

The same phenomenon occurs on a smaller scale in Western society too, when identity is conceived as something that is 'over against' other, more powerful subjects. The 'us and them' phenomenon can feed us, and make us resentful and angry. A victim mentality grows that shapes the secular soul, trapping it into a particular way of seeing the world, where nothing we do can change anything, and it is always someone else's fault that we cannot break out.[31]

The ideology of the extremist, growing up in a town in West Yorkshire, the young black person in Tottenham influenced by rap, the feminist railing against patriarchy, the young person, angry with his parents – the resentment of them all can be interpreted with Hegel's Master and Slave parable in mind. 'They fuck you up, your mum and dad', wrote Philip Larkin, memorably. His words of generational resentment recall Rousseau's words about freedom from the father, cited above. Such resentment takes hold easily today, and results in a sense of alienation between young person and parent, making parenting inordinately difficult. Many young people leave home, ready to transfer their anger and resentment onto others,

---

[31] Dalrymple, as he treats his patients in hospital and prison, describes how they will often talk as if they are the innocent victim of fate, using the passive tense. 'When a man tells me, in explanation of his anti-social behaviour, that he is easily led, I ask him whether he was ever easily led to study mathematics or the subjunctives of French verbs. Invariably the man begins to laugh: the absurdity of what he has said is immediately apparent to him. Indeed, he will acknowledge that he knew how absurd it was all along, but that certain advantages, both psychological and social, accrued by keeping the pretense [of victimhood] up.' *Life at the Bottom*, p. ix.

leading to cycles of grievance, and a sense of victimhood that entraps the person, and renders her unable to grow or flourish. Without forgiveness – of parents, for a start – that cycle does not break, but is repeated as the next generation is born. The secular soul hardens in resentment.

> *Mimi had put it as tactfully as she could, and had wanted Isabel to forgive her mother, which she had done, of course; forgiveness, Mimi pointed out, can be as powerful when it is posthumous as when it is given in life; perhaps even more so. This had intrigued Isabel, and she had realised that it was quite true: forgiveness of others allows us to adjust our feelings towards the past, assuages our anger. Our parents may disappoint us in so many ways: they could have done more, they made us neurotic, they should have insisted we learn the piano – and now it is too late; they were too strict, in big things or small; they were too poor, too ignorant, too rich and possessive. There are so many grudges we can hold against the past and for the love and approval that we did not get from it. But if we forgive, then the past can lose its power to hurt.*[32]

Identity politics feeds on resentment, and perpetrates it.

But instead of thinking of the human person as an identity, what happens if 'character' becomes the main category?

---

[32] McCall Smith, *The Charming Quirks of Others*, p. 127.

# 11

# *Character building*

Wright tells the story of the pilot who landed Flight 1549 on the Hudson River in January 2009. He describes how Captain Sullenburger and his co-pilot were able to respond in two or three minutes, completing complex actions necessary to save the plane, because of their training.

They had to shut down the engines. They had to set the right speed so the plane could glide as long as possible without power. They had to get the nose of the plane down to maintain speed. They had to disconnect the autopilot and override the flight management system. They had to activate the "ditch" system, which seals vents and valves, to make the plane as waterproof as possible once it hit the water. Most important of all, they had to fly and then glide the plane in a fast left-hand turn so that it could come down facing south, going with the flow of the river. And – having already turned off the engines – they had to do this using only the battery-operated systems and the emergency generator. Then they had to straighten the plane up from the tilt of the sharp-left turn so that, on landing, the plane would be exactly level from side to side.

Finally, they had to get the nose back up again, but not too far up, and land straight and flat on the water.[1]

The reason Sullenburger was able to do this was because his training had made such behaviour second nature. He did not have to think about it: it came naturally. Wright uses this as an illustration for how virtue can be acquired. We need to train ourselves, or be trained, to be virtuous. It does not just happen overnight.

This is a very different understanding of how we lead a good life, to that of the utilitarians, who argue that we should do that which has the consequence of the greatest happiness for the greatest number. To see virtue as something that needs to be worked at, practised so that it becomes customary and second nature, draws on a different strand of philosophical ethics.

## Endurance produces character

Wright argues that St Paul's letters are a good source of this sort of virtue ethics. Paul commended to the new Christians a way of life that was based on developing such qualities and virtues in themselves. It takes perseverance. It takes an understanding of suffering, for hard though it may be, suffering in life can help develop character. In Paul's letter to the Romans we remember that he writes this:

> ... we boast in our suffering, knowing that suffering produces endurance, and endurance produces character, and character produces hope, and hope does not disappoint us, because God's love has been pouring into our hearts through the Holy Spirit that has been given to us. (Rom. 5.3–5)

---

[1]  Tom Wright, *Virtue Reborn*, SPCK, London, 2010, pp. 7–8.

It is when we have to do something against our will that we discover what resources we have. That sense of discipline is there when we get ourselves out of bed, or away from the comfort of the TV in order to do something in the cold and wet, like play a team game, or visit someone who is lonely. It is in the actions of generosity towards others, when we are kind and gentle, that our character shows, and we become more human. Imitating others, whom we respect, has its effect upon us.[2]

## Growing in love

One of the limitations, when we see ourselves as 'identities', is that there is no way of accounting for how we might grow. It is a static term: once we have a particular identity, that is it. We cannot really grow any more in that identity. Once we have discovered we are gay, or come out as a gay person, we cannot become more gay. But we can become more kind. Loving-kindness. We can always become more kind, whoever we are.

Can we grow in love? This passage about love is perhaps the best-known in the Bible and suggests we can:

> If I speak in the tongues of mortals and of angels, but do not have love, I am a noisy gong or a clanging cymbal. And if I have prophetic powers, and understand all mysteries, and all knowledge, and if I have all faith, so as to remove mountains, but do not have love, I am nothing. If I give away all my possessions, and if I hand over my body so that I may boast, but do not have love, I am nothing.

---

[2] Patrick Gale's priest, Barnaby, carries *De Imitatione Christi* – *The Imitation of Christ* by Thomas a Kempis – with him wherever he goes, and models himself on what he reads from this Mediaeval manual for a monk.

Love is patient; love is kind; love is not envious or boastful or arrogant or rude. It does not insist on its own way; it is not irritable or resentful; it does not rejoice in wrongdoing, but rejoices in the truth. It bears all things, believes all things, hopes all things, endures all things.

Love never ends. But as for prophesies, they will come to an end; as for tongues, they will cease; as for knowledge, it will come to an end. For we know only in part, and we prophesy only in part; but when the complete comes, the partial will come to an end.

When I was a child, I spoke like a child, I thought like a child, I reasoned like a child; when I became an adult, I put an end to childish things. For now we see in a mirror, dimly, but then we will see face to face. Now I know only in part; then I will know fully, even as I have been fully known. And now faith, hope, and love abide, these three; and the greatest of these is love. (1 Cor., 13)

St Paul might almost have said 'If I have any number of identities, but do not have love, I am nothing'.

To cultivate a loving nature takes training. It takes practice not to be rude or arrogant, or resentful. Loving-kindness needs to be cultivated and its fruits become apparent in how we treat others.

*Good manners depended on paying moral attention to others; it required one to treat them with complete moral seriousness, to understand their feelings and their needs. Some people, the selfish, had no inclination to do this, and it always showed. They were impatient with those whom they thought did not count; the old, the inarticulate, the disadvantaged. The person with good manners, however, would always listen to such people and treat them with respect.*

*How utterly shortsighted we had been to listen to those who thought that manners were a bourgeois affectation, an irrelevance, which need no longer be valued. A moral disaster had ensued, because manners were the basic building block of civil society. They were the method of transmitting the message of moral consideration. In this way an entire generation had lost a vital piece of the moral jigsaw, and now we saw the results; a society in which nobody would help, nobody would feel for others; a society in which aggressive language and insensitivity were the norm.*

*She stopped herself. This was a train of thought which, though clearly correct, made her feel old; as old as Cicero declaiming O tempora! O mores! And this fact, in itself, demonstrated the subtle, corrosive power of relativism. The relativists had succeeded in so getting under our moral skins that their attitudes had become internalised, and Isabel Dalhousie, with all her interest in moral philosophy and distaste for the relativist position, actually felt embarrassed to be thinking such thoughts.*[3]

Good manners, which involve a sense of courtesy and behaviour that does not insist on its own way, need to be learned, and are best learned as we grow up in the home. The best manners are those that put others at ease: a warmth of smile, a kindness, gentleness and such things are universal, across all cultures. They may manifest themselves differently in different parts of the world, and then it is important to be sensitive and to learn the local expressions. If one is serious about being courteous, and one's efforts are received courteously, then if we go wrong, we will be forgiven. The old-fashioned attributes of a gentlewoman, or man, are perennial, and should be qualities, or virtues to aspire to, regardless of our 'identity'.

*A gentleman. Now that's a useful word, isn't it? And yet everybody's too embarrassed to use it these days, for some reason ... You get all*

---

[3] McCall Smith, *The Sunday Philosophy Club*, pp. 158–9.

*sorts of gentlemen. It doesn't matter where they're from or who they are. They're just gentlemen. You can trust them.*[4]

## An ethical turn

What motivates people to be good and kind? How can people, young and old, be encouraged to be generous and patient, and to put the needs of others before their own? To recognise self-centredness and self-interest for what they are? Moral sensibility happens when people grow into such things by experiencing them in society and in the Church, learning by the example set by others, and letting such virtues become second nature. To develop a sense of virtue is different to thinking that virtue is somehow there, already, intrinsic within you. Acquiring a virtuous character takes work, and the support and discipline of society, primarily within the family. Customs of good behaviour are best passed on from one generation to the next, and so they become second nature in society and in the individuals that belong to that society. And for a sense of character to develop, a person needs to be in an environment where a deliberative formation happens. That environment needs to be trustworthy, secure and positive: a given that we know we can trust, where our basic selfish nature is trained into a second nature.

## Character formed – and passed on – in the home

When I lived in Bradford, I would meet often with a close friend of mine. In the months before I moved, whenever Salima and I had some time with each other, one of the first topics of conversation has

---

[4] McCall Smith, *Friends, Lovers, Chocolate*, p. 181. Edmund Burke commented in *Letter to a Member of the National Assembly*, 1791, 'That a king may make a nobleman, but he cannot make a gentleman.'

been the progress of the arrangements for the marriage of her son. Tariq was bright, studying for a degree in politics and Islamic studies, aged 21 or so. With his parents, the decision was made that he felt ready to be married. To whom? Not, given Salima's anxieties about the effect of consanguineous marriages on the Muslim communities of Bradford, to any of his cousins, first, second or third. And nor was this in any way a 'forced' marriage, where the young woman would be compelled to marry someone against her choice.[5]

But it was important that she would come from a family with the similar values and take religion seriously; that she was bright and aspirational, with a love of education. Salima started to ask around within the community, and before long a family emerged. Then began a series of social meetings, of parents, with son and daughter. Their different characters were discussed in detail; compatibilities and non-compatibilities assessed. The two young people communicated by email, discussing any questions they might have of each other. It was a staged negotiation: either side could withdraw at any point.

After a month or so of meetings, and communication, Salima told me in great excitement that the decision was made; that the two were going to be married. I expressed my pleasure. 'Are you sure, though, Salima, that they didn't feel pressurised into it? Even really subtly?' 'No, honestly', came the reply. 'She is a strong young woman. She can say no'. 'Yes, she's going to need to be to take on Tariq, and you as a mother-in-law!' I said, and we laughed. Salima had plans that the newly-wed couple would live in an annexe of Salima and Amjad's new house for the first few years, until they find their feet.

This is an arranged marriage, by Islamically-faithful middle-class parents in Bradford, who take seriously the importance of

---

[5] See the film *Jasmin* for a realistic perspective of Islamic culture in West Yorkshire, post-9/11.

compatibility of character, value and aspiration, and family background in forming relationships that will last. This is different to other arranged marriages, though, in that 'keeping it in the family' is not a priority: Salima and her husband Amjad have seen enough from their own experience to want to avoid the practice of cousin-marriage that is common among the South-Asian-heritage communities around them.

One evening, we have a family meal together, Salima and Amjad, Peter and I and our children. Tariq is there, and he is the same age as our Jonty. On the way home, we discuss the arranged marriage. We considered whether, as white, Christian-heritage people we were missing something in our whole-hearted embrace of 'choice' based on romantic love. We wondered what it would be like if as parents we were more involved in choosing partners for our children, thinking carefully about character and compatibility. Jonty asked, seriously, which family we would turn to, if we were to follow the same practice. We had some moments of fun considering the options.

Of course, there are differences between us, Muslim and Christian, about what marriage is. Islamic marriage is a contract rather than a sacrament, which is how a Christian understands it. But with Salima and Amjad there was a much stronger grasp of what it might mean to manage the transitions from youth into adulthood with confident, hands-on parenting. They respected the needs and wishes of the young person, and this was appreciated. They did not shy away from offering the wisdom that can come with adult experience. Salima and Amjad gave guidance that relied upon a recognised and accepted moral framework that was rooted in their understanding of Islam. Such a moral framework is one in which their children are shaped and formed over time and it has much to recommend it.

Many Muslims like Salima and Amjad feel anxious about what they perceive to be a moral vacuum at the heart of Western civilisation. They are keen that their children grow up with the benefits of a traditional Islamic courtesy and ethical code of virtue, and we found, as our families met, that we valued many of the same qualities as each other. Christian and Muslim found common ground very easily, around key virtues of generosity and loving-kindness. But that anxiety about the moral vacuum at the heart of society is real, and has been described by others.

## A moral vacuum at the heart of society

Rowan Williams, in *Lost Icons*, traces how much has been lost from childhood. He describes how, in an instrumental, practical world, play is no longer seen as necessary in the onward march to attain skills and competencies. He grieves that the child has become a consumer, and therefore an economic subject,[6] vulnerable to market forces and advertising, rendered a pseudo-adult, with adult desires and pressures. If we recall how the romantic subject of the 1960s became fair game for shrewd capitalist opportunities, then the child now has been targeted too. And when his parents have already been trapped, and neither parent nor child has the cultural resources to escape that materialistic consumer pressure, then the child has little or no alternative. Williams believes, instead, that

> ... children need to be free of the pressures to make adult choices if they are ever to *learn* how to make adult choices. For them to be free for irresponsibility and fantasy, free from the commitments of purchasing and consuming, is for them to have time to absorb what is involved in adult choice. Failure to understand this is losing the very *concept* of childhood.[7]

---

[6] Rowan Williams, *Lost Icons: Reflections on Cultural Bereavement*, T&T Clark, Edinburgh and New York, 2000, p. 23, emphasis original.
[7] *Ibid.*, p. 27, emphasis original.

Children are like this too often, he says, because many adults have
never grown up, and have remained locked into childishness, uncom-
mitted and fantasy-driven. They 'can come to see themselves as *rivals*
in a single arena of competition'.[8] He says that 'the "safest" adult to
have around is one who is aware of having *grown* – one ... who knows
in his or her own experience how transitions are made from one sort
of choosing to another (which also means one who hasn't forgotten
what it is *like* to be a child)'.[9]

In mature adulthood, there is a clear distinction between child
and adult. There is not the infantilised competition that one often
sees in society today, where parent and child are locked into competition for material goods that somehow stand for love. To be a parent
is difficult, calling for a sense of right authority, which enables
discipline, but also forgiveness. Williams describes this growing in
maturity by talking about the soul, and the way it grows through
facing difficulty and contradiction. The soul needs time and patience
and the opportunities to worship '... a God who can't be negotiated
with, who has no interest to defend and whose creative activity is
therefore pure gratuity'.[10] Religion can offer into that toxic materialistic mix a different understanding of what it means to be human.
One which takes virtue seriously, and looks for trustworthy and
responsible character as the bedrock of the soul who is responsive to
God and to its neighbour.

## The moral habits of the heart

It should be clear by now that I am commending a way of being
human that discards 'identity' (except when we really need the word

---

[8] *Ibid.*, p. 28, emphasis original.
[9] *Ibid.*, p. 29, emphasis original.
[10] *Ibid.*, p. 162.

and none other will do), in favour of 'character'. Someone of character will work hard to grow within themselves moral habits that take seriously how we care for others around us. So when we see someone in need, our default position – because it is our second nature – is to go to help. And who is our neighbour? The lawyer asked Jesus. Jesus told the story of the Good Samaritan, illustrating his answer. Whoever is in need of help, regardless of their creed or culture or 'identity'.

## Revitalising civil society

How might society at large help families and individuals to develop character? To develop that second nature that turns us outward towards our neighbour and encourages us to think of public service as a good and worthwhile use of our time, energy and whatever other resources we have? A start might be to turn to the associations of civil society. I would suggest that civil society, being made up of associations and corporate groups that enable people to come together, enables the chance to volunteer or join an organisation that has goals beyond itself, thereby finding opportunities to serve others and so develop a sense of character. Edmund Burke called them 'little platoons' – a term which comes from a different age and sounds like it, but what he meant is still relevant today.

I also focus in this section on the importance of education to build resilience of character in Britain today, suggesting both that Church of England schools and colleges could become more explicit in the Christian virtues they encourage, and showcasing the example of Cathedral Choir schools which offer a different, traditional model of education to that dominant in contemporary culture.

# Little platoons

Robert Putnam brought 'civil society' into focus, with his *Bowling Alone*.[11] By 'civil society' is usually meant that arena which is outside of the state, the family and the market where people associate for common interests. Volunteering is an important aspect of this sphere: people contributing time and energy for the sake of the common good. Putnam highlighted the importance of the 'social capital' created by such association, and civil society has received a greater degree of attention, most notably, recently, by Jesse Norman and Phillip Blond. I want to suggest here that a healthy civil society strengthens society as a whole, and that the Church is woven into civil society in ways that continue to be resilient, offering 'little platoons' which could be further strengthened.[12]

Civil society. Civility and civilisation take their etymological root from the Latin for 'city', suggesting that as people live together a sense of community and common courtesy is important, if not essential, for the wellbeing of the society. Many of the organisations and associations that are there in civil society are traditional in this Burkean sense: they are properly constituted, with well-understood governance that ensures continuity and freedom from abuse. This

---

[11] See his *Bowling Alone: The Collapse and Revival of American Community*, New York, Simon and Schuster, 2000.

[12] See the General Synod report (January 2012) produced in response to the Church of England General Synod debate of November 2010 on the Big Society, entitled *Resourcing Christian Community Action: Parishes and Partnerships* in which a great many local projects are described extending throughout Britain. Professor Hilary Russell concludes by noting that the language of government is increasingly friendly towards the role of faith communities, but that there is 'a rising tide of need particularly among already vulnerable people in already deprived neighbourhoods and, on the other, tighter purse strings amongst potential funders of voluntary organisations, including church groups … The opportunities may be there to become more involved in service delivery but mainly without the resources to enable this to happen' p. 39.

structure of corporate life traces back to the guilds and associations of mediaeval society, as we saw when we examined the importance of the conciliar movement to the development of political history. There are many civil organisations and associations that already contribute much but could contribute more with the right support and greater encouragement.

Such voluntary bodies, charities, societies, associations, clubs and institutions are vulnerable though. Phillip Blond bemoans the passing of an age.

> We no longer have, in any effective independent way, local government, churches, trade unions, cooperative societies, publicly funded educational institutions, civic organisations or locally organised groups that operate on the basis of more than single issues. Whatever these various institutions represent now, what they embodied in the past were means for ordinary people to exercise power. These associations helped to give form and direction to human beings; they allowed parents to craft their families and citizens to shape their communities. Nowadays, however, all such sources of independent power have been eroded; instead, these civil spaces have either vanished or become subject-domains of the centralised state or the monopolised market.[13]

Is it so bleak?

I went recently to the Women's Institute (WI) near where I live. To my shame, it was the first time I had been to a WI meeting. After the business part, we listened to the speaker who talked about his experience of living in Rwanda. But before he talked, we sang *Jerusalem*. This WI sang beautifully, and I was moved. I had forgotten how Blake's words are remembered by women throughout the country.

---

[13] Blond, *op. cit.*, p. 3.

I shall not cease from mental fight
nor shall my sword sleep in my hand
Till we have built Jerusalem
in England's green and pleasant land.

The WI may not appeal to everyone, although since the film
*The Calendar Girls* the organisation has undergone something of
a makeover in the public eye. Such associations are invaluable
throughout Britain today. With their rituals, traditional governance
and outward-looking concern through charity to help others, groups
such as this enable people to belong, to be incorporated. The ritual
is important: when I went, the supper was eagerly awaited after
the speaker finished. And the governance is crucial to sustain the
continuity: the chair, the secretary, the agenda, the minutes, the
financial statement. Such practices ensure continuity, and a sense of
tradition within any association, and are extremely important to form
the corporate, ongoing life and sustainability of what is offered, both
in terms of fellowship and in enhancing the common good.

There are many other examples of such civil association, and
here I mention just a few. Credit Unions are growing in importance:
'The typical low-income household could save £500 a year in debt
repayments by borrowing money from a credit union', claims David
Lammy. Credit unions are owned by their members, in which savings
from some members are used to offer loans to others along the
cooperative model. To support credit unions, local authorities and
post offices around the country could offer office space, training and
help with back-office functions.[14] Building societies were established
on the same 'mutual' model, and the conversion of nearly all of them

---

[14] Lammy, *op. cit.*, p. 230.

to profit-making banks has arguably contributed significantly to the current economic situation.

Town or Street Pastors, or Angels, are currently emerging as a new movement taking place within the Churches in Britain. Having received training, and with codes of conduct in place, volunteer Christians from all denominations go out onto the streets of our towns and cities, generally on Friday and Saturday nights, working late into the small hours. They are often backed by a prayer team, which is there for as long as the Street Pastors are on the streets. Pairs of Christians go out caring for people on the streets. They defuse situations, protect the vulnerable and are a calming presence wherever they go. The benefits are not just felt by the clubbers and revellers, but the parents of young people also voice their support and appreciation that the care is taking place. In my local county, the Police in Suffolk have said that the current Town Pastor schemes in nine towns are now indispensable amidst the squalor and drunkenness, the vomit and disorder of town centres.

New initiatives, and older organisations all contribute to civil society – but many such associations fall foul of a current mindset that has decided that they are not fashionable or 'cool' to join (there is not the space to explore this phenomenon further here, but it is connected, I believe, to the culture of repudiation that I have described above, p. 57ff.). I think also of Rotary International, with its current target to eradicate polio from the world, and its ethos of international friendship. It is a highly impressive global civil organisation, but one which too often is repudiated in society at large. Western cultures, such as Britain, need to change their minds about volunteering and joining, for such organisations and associations strengthen civil society and are character-forming. They need to be supported, and encouraged; we need to change our national opinion about them, and see if we can make them attractive and inspiring again to new generations. For they enable civil society to happen.

'*Suspicion?*' *he asked. 'Are we more suspicious?*'

*Isabel had no doubts. 'Yes, of course we are. Look at airports –*
*you're a suspect the moment you set foot in one. And for obvious*
*reasons. But we're also more suspicious of everyone because we*
*don't know them any more. Our societies have become societies of*
*strangers – people with whom we share no common experience, who*
*may not speak the same language as we do. They certainly won't*
*know the same poems and the same books. What can you expect in*
*such circumstances? We're strangers to one another.'*

*Jamie listened intently. Yes, Isabel could be right, but where did*
*her observations take one? One could not turn the clock back to a*
*world where we all grew up in the same village.*

'*What can we do?*' *he asked.*

'*Nothing,' said Isabel. She thought for a moment about her*
*answer. It was defeatist, and it could not be right. We could seek*
*to recreate community, we could bring about a shared world of*
*cultural references and points of commonality. We had to do that,*
*or we would drift off into a separateness, which was almost where*
*we were now. But it would not be easy, this recreation of civil*
*society; it would not be easy taming the feral young, the gangs, the*
*children deprived of language and moral compass by neglect and*
*the absence of fathers. 'I don't really mean nothing,' she said. 'But*
*it's complicated.'*[15]

It is complicated. But it is enough to make a small step in the right
direction, and volunteering is something most people can offer in
however small a way. The culture of repudiation can be challenged
for it is often based on ignorance: it might not be cool to belong
to the Guides, or the Sea Cadets, but what they provide, in a safe

---

[15] McCall Smith, *The Careful Use of Compliments*, p. 130.

environment, is a real sense of adventure. It will be interesting to see if the Duchess of Cambridge will bring new glamour to the Scouts, now she is patron. The Duke of Edinburgh awards encourage young people to work together in character-forming situations: perhaps that experience could be continued beyond the goal of gaining the award for the school CV, enabling young people to take the opportunity to nurture personal growth and build a sense of belonging and trust in society.

It takes just a little imagination to change the culture – a little willingness to give something new a try – and there are countless opportunities out there in Western societies to get involved. I think of the example of Gareth Malone on the TV programme *The Choir*, and how he captured the imagination of people who would not normally think that they could sing, suggesting that the response is there to initiatives that bring people together. With his encouragement, the members of his choirs gain a voice, both literally and metaphorically, as they come together corporately to sing. Men Sheds are flourishing all over Australia and beginning to catch on in Britain too; another example of civil association that builds membership of the corporate, that reminds us not to be utilitarian and instrumental in our dealings with others, and that character is much more important than a shallow self-understanding of identity. Such belonging in civil associations nurtures the human soul. Churches are among the few organisations that bring together sizeable numbers of people for good. The organisation is there, and requires only imagination and initiative to do a little to enhance the common good. Renewed heart in the corporate association, nurturing a sense of virtue and character, could very quickly breathe vigour and enthusiasm back into Western culture.

# Philanthropy

Such association and voluntary work gives the opportunity for philanthropy, enabling those who are affluent to put something back into society. A sense of ethical accountability belongs to all who are members of the body of a society: rich and poor alike contribute to the common good. There are many who are rich who take seriously the promptings of a philanthropic motivation for the good of society as a whole, and are happy, enthusiastic even, to pay higher taxes, or to think seriously about being generous to help those who struggle. Learning about the plight of those who live in poverty and doing something long term and effective to help can be an obvious response to need. There is nothing wrong with wealth generation – it is crucial to a healthy economy. But when one is rich, it is easy to become disassociated from others in society, and lead to a sense of fearfulness, and the need to protect what one has. Wealth has its own traps. Greed can have an insidious effect on one's character and distort healthy relationships. Philanthropy can help to restore a sense of belonging, sparked in those who feel the need to give something back to society.

In many regions and counties, community foundations have been established that enable charitable giving and philanthropy to reach the neediest parts of the region in question. The Suffolk Foundation is one such organisation. It made its first grant in 2005 to the East Anglian Sailing Trust to support sailing for people with disabilities and their carers. Between 2005 and 2011 it awarded £4 million donated by individual philanthropists and funding partners to local charities and community groups, tackling social advantage in many forms: homelessness, rural isolation, domestic violence, addiction, disability, mental ill health, family difficulties. Working with organisations at the grass roots, such community foundations are strongly networked into local communities, the county council and the churches, offering a way to draw together the voluntary and community sector, and encouraging charitable giving and philanthropy.

## Where does trust begin?

Jonathan Sacks is the Chief Rabbi in Britain. He is also concerned about strengthening civil society. He asks 'How or where, though, does trust begin?' in society.[16] He draws a distinction between contractual relationships in society and those which are older and more organic. Many political and economic relationships are contractual, presupposing the coming together of self-interested parties, which enter it because they benefit from the exchange – such thinking, he argues (as I do) begins with Hobbes, Locke and Rousseau and the social contractual mindset we've identified above. Sacks suggests that we need to rediscover other ways of relating. He comments:

> Contractual relationships, however, are not the only or even the most fundamental forms of association. Consider, for example, the family: father, mother and children. They eat, drink, play and occasionally argue together. They take turns to do various chores. They have developed an unconscious choreography of mutuality. They help one another; they depend on one another; and that minuet of giving and taking is a not unimportant part of their identity and growth as individuals. They may have rules, which sometimes get broken. There are minor rebellions which are usually followed by rituals or reconciliation – someone says 'sorry', he or she is forgiven, and order is restored. Watching this microcosm of community and its everyday transactions, we see

[16] *The Dignity of Difference: How to Avoid the Clash of Civilizations*, Continuum, London and New York, 2002, pp. 148 ff. Rowan Williams explores the same issue in *Tokens of Trust*, *op. cit.*

something significant taking place: the making and sustaining of the moral life.[17]

Sacks explains that the same processes are there in civil associations where such making and sustaining of moral life is taken out of the family and into public life. He mentions Edmund Burke's 'little platoons' which, as we've seen, emerged from the pages of *Reflections*. Sacks asks, 'Where are they created? In families, communities, friendships, congregations, voluntary associations and fellowships of various kinds – in short, wherever people are brought together not by exchange of wealth or power but by commitment to one another or to a larger cause they serve in common'.[18]

Whether or not the rhetoric of 'the Big Society' means anything, something along its lines is required – a strengthening of civil society. This will only happen if there is a conscious and deliberate valuing of the associations – the 'little platoons' – of civic society. Too often the rhetoric of the Big Society becomes instrumental: what can the Churches deliver? How can this or that organisation step up to fill the gaps left by a retreating state? That is not the way. Instead, central government could make it easier to belong to such associations by reducing the amount of regulations and legislation that put off so many people from volunteering. Those in leadership roles can talk more fulsomely about civil association, to change the culture of repudiation that makes joining and belonging so difficult for many, both young and old. Civil society needs to be valued as an end in itself; the place where individuals can come together to contribute to the common good in many and varied ways, building the corporate moral life, and a sense of individual and national character.

---

[17] *Ibid.*, p. 149.
[18] *Ibid.*, p. 152.

# 12

# *The role of education*

Earlier I analysed the narcissism that leaves us too vulnerable to market forces, as we compete for material goods because that is often the only way we can express any sense of worth. The cultural impoverishment of a society that is overly materialistic is a tragedy, I believe, and in this section we explore how young people might be encouraged to build internal resources to enable them to resist the pressures that turn them into fodder for ever-inventive market forces. How might young people receive a different diet to 'the pursuit of happiness' that makes them vulnerable to whatever the market dictates – the latest fashion, the newest this, the must-have that? How do we, as a society, enable young people to grow in a sense of dignity, of emotional and moral maturity? Culturally enriched, with human souls?

## Ideological tensions

The tensions between Rousseau and Burke can be seen here, if we look at how contemporary education has developed since the ideological revolution of the 1960s and 1970s. With broad brushstrokes – but speaking for many with his analysis – Andrew Marr charts the history of the introduction of comprehensive schooling in Britain in the 1970s. Begun by Anthony Crosland in the Labour years, it was completed when Margaret Thatcher was Education Secretary, despite her declared enthusiasm for grammar schools. Marr comments that it was unfortunate that the comprehensive experiment coincided with a move away from traditional education to what was called 'child-centred teaching', and it was this, he believes, rather than the introduction of comprehensive education as such, that so undermined education.

> It was the singular misfortune of the comprehensive experiment that it coincided with a move away from traditional education to what was called child-centred teaching. In the long run, this may well have been more important than structural reorganisation of schools. Instead of viewing the child as an empty pot, happily large or sadly small, into which a given quantity of facts and values could be poured, the new teaching regarded the child as a magic box, crammed with integrity and surprise, which should be carefully unwrapped ... Here was a fundamental disagreement about the nature of humanity and social order. Philosophically it goes back to the French thinkers of the eighteenth century but it was fought out in concrete form in British classrooms throughout this period. The old rows of desks facing a blackboard began to go, and cosily intimate semicircles of chairs appeared. Children of different abilities were taught in the same room, so that they could learn from each other, causing some chaos and boredom. Topics replaced lists. Grammar retreated and creativity advanced. Teachers began to dress informally and encouraged the use of an Adrian or Sara, rather than Sir or Miss. Corporal punishment went from state schools entirely and on the vast, windy sites of the seventies comprehensives, with their modernist airiness, discipline loosened. The elite remained mainly in private

schools, taught much as their parents and grandparents had been. But across the country millions of parents shook their heads and wondered. Hostility to comprehensives, which would swell through the eighties and nineties, was much of the time really hostility to trendy teaching, the spirit of the sixties which was being marshalled and organised in scores of teacher training colleges.[19]

We know, because we have already examined Rousseau's thought, which eighteenth century French philosopher Marr has in mind here, and we see here how the romantic impulse of the 1960s gained an ideological grip on educationalists. Comprehensive schools are often in the glare of criticism, but Marr suggests, and I would agree with him, that it was the ideology that came in at the same time which left much to be desired, not the principle of comprehensive education in itself. This ideology was the almost inevitable outcome of the 1960s, and went hand in hand with Rousseau's idea of freedom from the constraints of parents, schools, traditions and old ways of doing things. Many have argued that the notion, and ideology, of child-centred education first came to light with the 1967 Plowden Report on primary school education. Plowden drew heavily on the psychology of Jean Piaget, and the report's now-famous opening passage had a profound influence on subsequent educational theory, putting, as it does, the nature of the child at the centre:

> At the heart of the educational process lies the child. No advances in policy, no acquisitions of new equipment have their desired effect unless they are in harmony with the nature of the child, unless they are fundamentally acceptable to him. We know a little about what happens to the child who is deprived of the stimuli of

---

[19] Marr, *A History of Modern Britain*, pp. 249–50.

pictures, books and spoken words; we know much less about what happens to a child who is exposed to stimuli which are perceptually, intellectually or emotionally inappropriate to his age, his state of development, or the sort of individual he is. We are still far from knowing how best to identify in an individual child the first flicker of a new intellectual or emotional awareness, the first readiness to embrace new sets of concepts or to enter into new relations.[20]

The secular soul was born and its education determined by what was intellectually or emotionally appropriate to the child's age, state of development and sort of individual he was. The horizons began to shrink; no longer was it appropriate to introduce the child to knowledge that was far beyond the utmost bounds of human thought, giving resources that would grow with the child as the child grew in response to the challenge of an education that always suggested there was more to learn and know of the best that has been thought and said. Modern education had arrived, with all its utopian visions for the future, expressed in new architecture, new methods, new styles, and a new concept of the child. Here was, indeed, a fundamental revolution about the nature of humanity and social order. Woodhead says this:

> To allow children to remain ignorant of, say, literature, history or mathematics is to deny them the inheritance upon which their humanity depends. The teacher's task is not to collude in the nonsense of personalisation. It is to encourage a willingness to submit to a body of knowledge which has, with patience and humility, to be mastered.[21]

---

[20] The Plowden Report (1967), Children and their Primary Schools, A Report of the Central Advisory Council for Education (England), London, Her Majesty's Stationery Office.

[21] Woodhead, *op. cit.*, pp. 99–100 . He argues, convincingly, that the academic standards of children have fallen since the 1960s, and illustrates his case with reference to exam papers.

There is something to be said, I think, for re-examining some of this ground, and reconsidering what traditional models of education bring to the table. Fifty years on since that social revolution, I wonder how much 'child-centred' education has contributed to the narcissism that so many commentators suggest is part of what makes Western culture so brittle today. I know education theory has moved on from some of the wackier ideas, but I also know that the 'individual child' is still at the centre of thinking. A shift of perspective is needed, with a re-appraisal of what a more traditional model of education might offer. I am not, I re-iterate, advocating the suppression of the individual, but rather that he finds his proper place as part of a corporate identity, and a heritage of learning and knowledge, that allows his unique individuality and humanity to flourish.

## Benedictine roots: a school of the Lord's service

We propose, therefore, to establish a school of the Lord's service, and in setting it up we hope we shall lay down nothing that is harsh or hard to bear. But if for adequate reason, for the correction of faults or the preservation of charity, some degree of restraint is laid down, do not then and there be overcome with terror, and run away from the way of salvation, for its beginning must needs be difficult. On the contrary, through the continual practice of monastic observance and the life of faith, our hearts are opened wide, and the way of God's commandments is run in a sweetness of love that is beyond words. Let us then never withdraw from discipleship to him, but persevering in his teaching in the monastery till death, let us share the sufferings of Christ through patience, and so deserve also to share in his kingdom.

In 480 a man was born in Italy who was to have an inestimable influence on the development of Western civilisation. As the late Roman Empire crumbled under the onslaught of wave after wave of attack from the tribes of surrounding lands, St Benedict founded a monastery at Mount Cassino and lived there with monks who followed the rule he wrote. From there his monastic rule travelled throughout Western Christendom, where it gave the basis as communities were established, often in isolated places, but which have continued and survived as towns and cities throughout Europe. The Rule of St Benedict inspired the communities that founded many of the Cathedrals of Europe, and throughout the Middle Ages such settlements were often havens of stability and continuity in a world of disorder and uncertainty. This rule continues to be followed today, as it has been for 1,500 years. These words above come from the Prologue of the Rule of St Benedict. They introduce a short document that is gentle and wise in its instruction, with a profound understanding of human nature and what is required to enable people to live together and belong corporately.

Monastic life was based upon virtues that took discipline and time to acquire, but which bore real fruit in terms of the formation of souls – individuals who knew what it mean to belong to the particular corporate life of a particular monastic community. Life there took shape through prayer, through reading and intellectual study, and through physical work, all to the end of glorifying God. The psalms and scriptures would be learned by heart, inwardly digested to feed the soul. The Benedictine way of life provided, all those years ago, and up to the present time, the most enduring and resilient school, and was often at the forefront of education, recognising its civilising effect on the surrounding population.

Benedictine monks and nuns took, and still take, three vows. The vow of stability means a commitment to a particular monastic community. Benedict advised against the monks who would wander from monastery to monastery, never stopping long enough to put roots down and learn about themselves through commitment to others. Loyalty to the particular people around the monk was important, involved with others, and receiving support from them was part of the formative process. The second vow is called the vow of the conversion of manners, or life, which means that the monk commits himself to live as a celibate and to renounce personal ownership. Celibacy was part – but only a part – of the adoption of a virtuous life and the promise to go on trying throughout his life to become better and more wholehearted in his service of God. Renouncing personal ownership meant that all things were held in common, following the injunction in the Acts of the Apostles. The third vow is a vow of obedience. Obedience was due to the Abbot, but also to other monks, preventing the monk from becoming personally ambitious, self-willed and domineering, and enabling him to imitate the humility of Jesus Christ. This way of life is followed by men and women throughout the world, both Roman Catholic and Anglican, living in convents and monasteries. This religious order has had, and still has a particular commitment to education.

For those not called to the monastic life, the Rule of St Benedict can still offer an understanding of the virtuous life, as many are exploring today. Qualities such as stability and continuity, the formation of character, commitment to community and humility characterise the spirit of Benedict as it is applied to different contexts and walks of life. Throughout the Rule the emphasis is upon gentleness and not pushing the monks too hard, but enabling them to learn stability, a sense of personal discipline, and how to love God and love their neighbour. There is not the space here to offer a thorough exploration of the ways in which a Benedictine spirituality might inform educational theory and practice for today's world, but it would be instructive to do so. Many Roman Catholic faith schools continue to benefit from the ethos that St Benedict's rule provides, with an explicit formative culture that offers something distinctive to the children that is different to the educational ideology of the state system, based upon liberal egalitarian principles.

These are deep roots that stretch back through Western society to its earliest days and throughout the centuries, education has been at the heart of the Benedictine way of life. You see it most clearly as it survives in Cathedral Choir schools today.

## Standing in surroundings I could once not have dreamed of

A different pedagogy has survived in Cathedral Choir schools, providing education which has different goals to that informed by a child-centred ideology. The whole purpose of a Cathedral choir is to continue a tradition of choral music that extends back to the beginnings of the Benedictine way of life in the early 5th century, when singing was introduced to enhance worship as an offering to God. And so the child who becomes a chorister today quickly learns that the purpose of singing is to learn and perform to the best of her ability, to enhance the worship that is offered to God. The chorister is nurtured, and his abilities are drawn out appropriately to his maturity, but he is not at the centre of his learning, because the needs of the choir as it fulfils its end of singing to the glory of God are more important than him or any other individual.

David Lammy MP talks of his training as a chorister at Peterborough Cathedral.

I will always remember appearing on Songs of Praise when it was held in Peterborough Cathedral. I was given the opportunity to sing some of the greatest music ever produced, standing in surroundings I could once not have dreamed of, with my voice being broadcast across the UK. I could visualise my family setting the VCR at home in Tottenham after spending most of the week reminding colleagues and neighbours about my appearance. I was overwhelmed by pride. It was not for a prize, a record contract or a financial reward, but simply for what I was doing. I experienced, for perhaps the first time, the transcendence of applying myself completely to something. This was what I understood aspiration to mean: the urge to learn a craft, to do something brilliantly, to fulfil a talent through hard work.[22]

## The Anglican choral tradition

Lammy's experience of hard work for the reward of singing 'some of the greatest music ever produced' is shared by many young boys and girls in the Anglican Cathedrals around the world.[23] Young people start from about the age of seven. Some come from very disadvantaged backgrounds. They learn to be disciplined and that what they are offering is part of a tradition that stretches back centuries, into the Benedictine monastic foundation that predated Cathedral life. The musical education they receive is choir-centred: the children quickly learn that if they don't turn up, then the whole choir suffers. They are necessary, but ultimately this is not about them, but about their contribution to the whole. On the way, over the years, they learn

---

[22] Lammy, *op. cit.*, p. 132.

[23] Michael White wrote this recently of choral evensong: 'Calm apart, what choral evensong achieves – apart from pleasing God, which figures somewhere in the rationale – is to declare the Church of England's role as one of the great vocal factories of all time. Since the Reformation, but particularly since the early 20th Century, it's produced a singing culture like no other.' "Lift up your voices for our brilliant British choirs," in *Daily Telegraph*, 3 December 2011.

a wide range of music; some of it very difficult. Much is expected of them, and they respond, to a high standard that does justice to them and to what the Cathedral offers to God in worship. Often they do not come from church-going families, but they learn not only to sing, but are also introduced to those virtues of Christianity that St Paul outlined: self-control, forgiveness, gentleness. Many go on to sing as adults, girls and boys, after their voices have matured or broken, to provide alto, tenor and bass lines. They have received tools of learning that stand them in good stead in other areas of their lives and education.

So here children gain an education that is not about acquiring utilitarian skills for the workforce, transferable competencies that can be ticked off. This education is not about passing tests and exams in formulaic ways, by producing required, pre-digested gobbets of knowledge that make the tests easy to mark. This is not tasting different topics, and then moving on to the next. The education of a chorister introduces the child to difficult and challenging material, and over a number of years, that music becomes known intimately. It is an education that has given Britain the best choirs, arguably, in the world. Those who run cathedral choirs assume that children are capable of more than we think.

Cathedral choirs are living illustrations of the spirit of St Benedict. They require a level of commitment and discipline that from the outset is determined by the needs of the choral tradition itself. In order to be able to sing this music to the required standard, steady, regular attendance is required at rehearsal, day in, day out, throughout the year. The intensity of learning is high; much is expected of young children. They are trained to perform, with excellence, to do justice to the living tradition that they have inherited and which is their responsibility to pass on to future generations. The individuality of each child is crucial, for each brings something unique, but this education is not individualistic, but corporate. It is corporate because of the choir continues from the past, through the present and into the future, a distinctive body that transcends present time and space, with memory of what has gone before, and bearing hope for what the future brings. That continuity, and sense of the long term, creates stability, and is Benedictine in spirit.

The music has stood the test of time: each individual becomes part of a tradition of excellence that is challenging to master and sophisticated in execution, written originally and performed through the years in order to perform to enable others to worship, and to the glory of God. It is a choral tradition that is added to in every generation, but only the best stands the test of time. The anthems and chants, from all centuries since the Early Church, are learned off by heart and continue in that person's repertoire into adulthood, providing a resource of beauty and enduring aesthetic value, giving the child an artistic inheritance of emotional and moral depth that grows with the child as she matures.

It is a different model of education to that in many schools. The goals are different: there are no targets and outcomes to meet when a Cathedral choir sings Choral Evensong. Learning is not reduced to bite-size chunks, but is a rich feast that takes years to digest. The individual child and her self-realisation is not as important as the excellence of the choir, and so some degree of self-sacrifice is called for by each member, forgoing individual wants and desires for the good of the whole. Cathedral choirs offer a good example of an education which is corporate, rather than individualistic, that is non-instrumental and which is concerned with character. The spirit of Benedict continues as choirs sing evensong, daily, in Anglican Cathedrals across the world.

# Church of England schools and colleges

The Anglican Church has always taken its commitment to education seriously – around the globe and in England, particularly since 1811, when the National Society was founded, and the Church of England first promoted 'the education of the poor in the principles of the established church'. Church of England schools are not faith schools, narrowly understood. The key distinction between Church of England schools and faith schools (whether, for example, Roman Catholic, Jewish or Muslim) is that church schools see it as their role to educate children from all backgrounds in the neighbourhood, functioning as centres of reconciliation among people of different races and creeds, whereas faith schools tend to enrol children who belong distinctly to the faith in question. The commitment of the National Society to schooling in the poorest communities was one of the central priorities taken forward into the comprehensive vision.

By the time of the 1944 Education Act, a large proportion of the nation's schools were church owned and run. This act set out to reform the educational system after the Second World War, to provide secondary education for all children. Church schools became either voluntary-controlled or voluntary-aided – categories that exist to this day, designating two different levels of local parish and diocesan responsibility for the financial and governance provision alongside the Local Education Authority. School worship was made obligatory in all state maintained schools; religious instruction obligatory in all county schools in accordance with a locally agreed syllabus.

During the 1980s and 1990s there was a plethora of Education Acts, and continuing debate about the role of religion in education, which continues at the present time. In an increasingly secular age, the question of the extent to which education should be 'religious' and what that means is never far away from consideration, and has become of particular interest as other faiths have claimed the right to have state-sponsored faith schools. These questions continue to be lively as we embark upon a time of educational reform under the current coalition government. One of the real pressures upon Church of England schools today is to sacrifice the commitment to the education of the poorest of our society in their own localities in pursuit of league table success to meet the expectations of middle-class families who will often move into particular areas because of the Anglican schooling available. Plans to introduce academies and free schools will only exacerbate this trend, I fear. But, as I mentioned earlier, poverty is not only a material concept, and Church of England schools and colleges can do much to provide a culturally enriching education that challenges the cultural impoverishment that affects all classes in Western societies.

A Salvation Army friend once commented to me that the Anglican Church doesn't realise sufficiently what a resource it has in its schools and colleges, and what difference they could make to Britain. The Church of England should be much bolder, much more distinctive, she argued. The remark has remained with me. I wonder if the Church of England could offer more through its schools and colleges to nurture a stronger sense of resilience within the children who attend to enable them to grow into *homo sapiens*, rather than *homo economicus*. Certainly I know Salima and Amjad would welcome this: they, like many Muslim parents, prefer Church schools for their children, suspicious of what they perceive to be the moral vacuum of state schools. (They would also welcome a greater integration between statutory education and madrassah education, but that idea will need to wait for another day.) Using the spirit of Benedict imaginatively is one way in which the Christian ethos and culture of Church of England schools and colleges could be enhanced.

## The benefits of a religious outlook

There is a difference between teaching, or learning about, religion and experiencing it. A phenomenological approach to learning about different religions is important in today's world. But so is absorbing the benefits of a religious outlook as a way of life, a practice and set of beliefs, for it provides different ways of knowing and things to know.[24] If a Benedictine spirit were to inform Anglican Church schools and colleges more widely, children would absorb that sense of continuity and stability, of humility, of an education for its own sake, rather than to fulfil the requirements of an instrumental and utilitarian mindset. They would gain a different understanding of how to treat people – with self-sacrifice, rather than self-interest, and grow with a sense of their own individuality formed within a first-person plural, rather than first-person singular culture. They would receive a wise religious upbringing that would help them grow into *homo sapiens*, with human souls.

Much of this goes on already in Church of England schools and colleges, and is a reason for their continuing popularity. They offer a distinctive culture, which is inclusive and non-proselytising. This culture could be enhanced, offering a more explicit emphasis upon the development of virtues, such as those outlined in St Paul's letter to the Galatians: love, joy, peace, patience, faithfulness, gentleness,

---

[24] Woodhead describes the difference as he looks back to his Grammar School education like this: 'Time was not wasted on citizenship and PSHE (personal, social, health education) lessons. The understandings and values these pseudo-subjects now struggle to make explicit were embedded in the everyday fabric of the school and were transmitted all the more effectively because of that' *op. cit.*, p. 7.

kindness, generosity, self-control and a constant encouragement to develop a character based upon these nine Christian virtues. With a school ethos of virtue and character building, drawing on the Benedictine tradition the culture of the school would be such that the more formal aspects of teaching would happen in a milieu in which each child would be encouraged to consider the common good, what sort of society they wanted to live in, and how they might contribute positively to it, as public servants of the future.

In Church of England schools and colleges, with an enhanced Christian culture, children of other faiths would be encouraged to contribute from their own perspectives, and a strong sense of the common ground of religion is emphasised. Children need clear boundaries and direction about what is acceptable behaviour and what is not, and discipline would need to be understood as a formative process, guiding and developing a sense of character with the focus on the child's own sense of self-control. The education offered here could be more strongly rooted in the Christian practice of forgiveness: children enabled to learn that it is all right to fail; that saying 'sorry' is important and necessary if one is to learn how to live with others. The individualistic 'child-centred' ideology could be countered by encouraging children not to think of themselves as 'I' foremost, but as 'we'; and this imbued by a greater emphasis on choirs, sports teams and different group activities.

Nothing here is revolutionary stuff; merely that the distinctive Christian ethos could be strengthened and made much more explicit. For example, all the Church of England schools I have been involved with have taken the Golden Rule as the main ethical basis: to treat others as you would like to be treated. Christian virtues are more explicit about reaching out to others in ways that put them first, rather than self. Self is decentred as one learns to love one's neighbour, in a way that does not happen with the Golden Rule, which can merely mean that the individual behaves passively, in accordance with the prevailing culture. If you are brought up with cruelty, then too often cruelty becomes normal, and treating others as you would want to be treated becomes degraded to treating others as you are treated. There is no real encouragement to learn to be different by moving outwards to the other, away from self, and eventually experiencing the costs and demands of the moral claims of one's neighbour.

## A nudge towards a Christian ethic

To enhance the acquisition of virtue and the development of character, projects could be introduced that present such ideas positively, and use the ideas of 'Nudge'.[25] For example, Church of England primary schools might develop a scheme entitled 'Telling Tales of Kindness'. Children could be encouraged to tell tales of times when they have seen kindness, or patience, or self-control, or generosity between their peers, with appropriate affirmation for both the tale teller and the good behaviour. This would ensure a positive nudge towards a Christian ethic which puts love of neighbour, and kindness at the heart of what it means to be human. The emphasis, over time, would be away from a vigilant detection of bullying and towards creating a much stronger culture where bullying would become less likely as the children learned positive ways of behaving.

The great strength of Church of England schools and colleges is the ethos they provide, in all areas of the country, traditionally with a particular emphasis on poor communities. That Christian

---

[25] Cass Sunstein and Richard Thaler, *Nudge: Improving Decisions about Health, Wealth and Happiness,* Yale University Press, London, 2008.

culture could be strengthened and made more explicit, very easily, I believe, and a real difference to society could result, enabling children to grow more able to cope with the challenges of the hedonism and narcissism of a brittle age. There would be other advantages, too. The evident lack of religious literacy amongst those currently in public service and generally in society would be addressed by a more explicit experience of Christianity in practice, received at school. If then, subsequently, the religious outlook is rejected, at least it would be on the basis of some knowledge, not ignorance.

I have concentrated on Church of England schools and colleges, and Cathedral Choir schools; the first because these schools offer a unique opportunity to enhance what the Church offers society, enabling children to build a sense of character than helps them to be resilient as they grow to face the pressures and challenges of adult life with emotional and moral maturity. I have described the virtues that come from the Benedictine tradition, and have argued that Cathedral Choir schools offer a model of education that belongs within this tradition, extending back and surviving the ideological waves of the 1970s. Instead of an education where the child is put at the centre, in an 'every child matters' way, with an emphasis on the individual and his acquisition of skills and competencies that will equip him for the world of work, such an educational approach might offer something very different, where rich cultural knowledge is gained by heart, to support an emotional and moral development towards and through adulthood.

The benefits of this approach could have a positive impact by providing more music in schools generally in the UK. Jesse Norman wants to see children receiving much more music in schools. He bemoans the fact that millions of young people, especially from the poorest and most disadvantaged families, have had limited access to or enjoyment of playing music. He talks about 'futile culture wars'[26] which label classical music as 'an elitist activity only open to the wealthy few, rather than a massively empowering activity for the many'. The experience of Cathedral music schools and departments is that those who become choristers are empowered by the experience. If schools generally are to be more involved in encouraging and promoting musicality, I would suggest that Cathedrals have much to contribute to society as a whole, and if, as Norman suggests, it would not take a great deal of funding to resource music education properly, across Britain, there are resources here to draw upon.[27] It is worth noting that one of the striking characteristics of cathedral schools – only one of which, at Westminster Abbey, nowadays comprises only choristers – is the way in which almost all pupils are encouraged and enabled to take part in music-making, and not only of the classical variety.

We began this section asking how a society can encourage young people to build internal resources to enable them to resist the pressures of a narcissistic age, so that elusive happiness does not become their only goal in life, and so that they grow with a sense of dignity and emotional and moral maturity rather than an 'us and them' identity

---

[26] Norman writes: 'These culture wars have been buttressed by a mythology of talent and "genius" which suggests that only a few people have the requisite ability to play; when in fact the truth is that almost everyone has musical ability, but that hard work and focused practice are what really matters. Within music education itself there has been a long and unhelpful stand-off between advocates of classical music and others who are equally passionate about world music, jazz and other forms. There remain music services across the country, but they are struggling to make ends meet as these and other factors undermine popular understanding of and belief in music' *op. cit.*, p. 211.

[27] He suggests £60–£80 million a year to cover all primary and secondary schools, plus orchestras. He says that it's a very modest amount; roughly half the average *daily* interest payment on our current fiscal deficit. *Ibid.*, p. 212. The 'Sing-Up' Chorister Outreach Programme of 2008 was a tremendous initiative and shows just how much appetite there is for the development of music in young people.

that fosters resentment and grievance. In short, growing into adults who are not culturally impoverished, but who have a strong sense of gratitude for the gifts of life, of joy, with personality, character and responsibility in the world, motivated by the desire to put the needs of others above self and committed to the common good.

# Conclusion

Having examined something of the philosophical roots of the notion 'identity', I have tried to draw out some of the places where a sense of character based upon the Christian injunction to love God and love your neighbour can be developed. I have suggested that civil society is crucial to this, and we have looked at the ways in which civil association might be enhanced through different traditional and more contemporary ways. I have suggested that Cathedral Choir schools provide a traditional education, with its roots in a Benedictine monasticism that survived the ideological revolution of the 1970s. With this in mind, I have considered how Church of England schools and colleges might offer a stronger moral environment and religious framework, to develop a sense of character, and have looked at what the Benedictine tradition might offer as resources to that end.

We have now covered the ground that this book set out to map. We have traced the roots of three aspects of the secular soul – its excessive individualism, its preoccupation with an instrumental and utilitarian mindset, and its insistence of having an 'identity'. In an age which many call narcissistic, it is important to talk about being corporate, where proper individuality is found in belonging to the body, with all our differences, gifts and failings. Seeing each other as ends, rather than means to our selfish goals, hints that we might ourselves need to find our end in something beyond the contingencies of human existence, and we have explored the divine realm of worship, where we find meaning in a different space and time. The shallow notion of 'identity' has been unmasked to reveal resentment and tribal belonging. The human soul, full of character, has so much more to give, especially when virtues become second nature.

# *Conclusion*

What does Christianity have to offer in today's world? Many have concluded that religion, and Christianity in particular, has had a poisonous impact upon the development of Western culture. Such people say that those few adherents who still follow Jesus Christ are blinded by a wilful irrationality and have failed to grasp the benefits of the Enlightenment. A world without God is a better world: a secular world does not need a God to shore up morality or to provide false myths instead of the truths of scientific knowledge. Humanity is quite capable of living the good life without God: it has a secular soul, if it has one at all, a soul that finds fulfilment in self-actualisation.

I have put a different case here. I have commended Christianity as a power for good throughout the centuries, politically, aesthetically and morally. Rather than present a Christianity that is hamstrung by guilt for the past (although, of course, it has been responsible for its fair share of hypocrisies, atrocities and failures), I have argued that Christianity shapes the human soul positively: away from excessive individualism and into a true individuality that comes when we know ourselves, first and foremost, to be social beings; away from an instrumental, utilitarian mindset, and towards the enjoyment of things, people and God as ends in themselves; and away from the notion of 'identity' ubiquitous in society today, towards the second nature that comes as we acquire a virtuous character. In short, I have contended that human beings do have souls, and that they are best nurtured on the rich feast that Christianity provides, rather than the thin gruel of secular humanism.

I have shown the philosophical antecedents of each of the three themes – excessive individualism, utilitarian and instrumental rationality, the concept of 'identity' – as we have focused on Jean-Jacques Rousseau, Jeremy Bentham and then a trajectory that began with Hegel's parable of the Master/Slave dynamic. As such ideas have grown in ascendancy they have eclipsed the more traditional understanding of the human being and society that has developed over the centuries in Christian theology and philosophy, with its central concern for how people might live as the people of God, both in the Church and in society, loving their neighbours and giving of self to enhance the common good. Christianity has long been concerned with education, enabling people to grow in emotional and moral knowledge to equip them to cope with the pressures of life, and the losses that inevitably come their way. We have explored what the loss of Christianity might entail for Western culture, and how shallow and vacuous life can become without the rich story of the life, death and resurrection of Jesus Christ.

I have drawn on the thought of Edmund Burke in the belief that his commendation of tradition, and the 'little platoons' of civic association have much to teach us today. I believe he should be more widely read than he is.[1] His defence of constitutional monarchy assumed the existence of God, whose authority undergirds society. I have suggested that without that sense of divine authority, we are left with only democracy as a source of political power. I have expressed concern that without the counter balances that come through other

---

[1] Why is he not remembered, for instance, in the Anglican Calendar for his contribution to political and social thought?

sources of legitimate authority, mediated through the House of Lords, where a majority are appointed because of merit, and mediated by the crown, British society becomes weakened and vulnerable to the abuses of arbitrary power exercised by absolute democracy.

We have returned again and again to the central actions of the Church in its liturgy, where those who participate make a journey that enables them to find their humanity and flourish, learning how to forgive and love their neighbours, learning how to be self-sacrificial rather than self-interested, and learning what the mandate to be the Body of Christ means. I have commended worship as a time and space where it is possible to be a true individual, indivisible from the corporate body which is the social to which we all belong. I have said that worship offers the opportunity to play and reflect upon our lives, to encounter fear and to grow in wisdom, to develop a moral and emotional knowledge that gives us the resources to cope with the vicissitudes and losses that we inevitably encounter in life.

I have also explored how church-going, civil association and education can enable us to grow out of our 'identity' and shape a sense of character, based upon the virtues that are at the heart of the Christian way of life. I have suggested that St Paul's letters and the Rule of St Benedict offer rich material for a deeper theological understanding of what Jesus Christ taught, and what he gave in his birth, life and death. I have attempted to show what an alternative might be to the secular soul which currently is so prevalent in Western societies today. I have described the Christian formation that has been foundational to our society and which still has deep wellsprings, but which is fragile. I have expressed my hope that my agnostic readers might explore their doubts properly by the practice of regular church-going, and that the benefits of so doing are unknowable until that practice has become habitual. As David Bentley Hart has said, the only really honest way to know what one is dismissing is to practise, and pray. At least then one knows, from the inside, what one is rejecting.

I have argued that often belief follows the practice of worship, and have commended the Anglican Church and church-going throughout this book to nourish the human soul. I have come to believe through the practice of church-going, that Christianity offers the best revelation of God in the birth, life, death and resurrection of Jesus Christ, and that following his way is the most fruitful and satisfying course that any human person can take through life. But, of course, the proof of that pudding is in the eating.

## The art of gratitude

In the series, set in Edinburgh, which begins with *The Sunday Philosophy Club*, Alexander McCall Smith has created Isabel Dalhousie. Isabel is a moral philosopher with a creative mind. She muses to herself and has interesting conversations with friends. With her author's permission, I have woven those musings into this book, where they have, I hope, lifted my argument and enriched the text.

Let us suppose that Isabel Dalhousie decides to leave her house early one Sunday morning, and to take herself along to an Episcopal Church service, perhaps at St John's, on Princes Street. What might she find? It would be Holy Communion according to the Book of Common Prayer. Hopefully she would hear the priest say this prayer, after communion.

> Almighty and everliving God, we most heartily thank thee, for that thou dost vouchsafe to feed us, who have duly received these holy mysteries, with the spiritual food of the most precious Body and Blood of thy Son our Saviour Jesus Christ; and dost assure us thereby of thy favour and goodness towards us; and that we are very members incorporate in the mystical body of thy Son, which

is the blessed company of all faithful people; and are also heirs through hope of thy everlasting kingdom, by the merits of the most precious death and passion of thy dear Son. And we most humbly beseech thee, O heavenly Father, so to assist us with thy grace, that we may continue in that holy fellowship, and do all such good works as thou has prepared for us to walk in; through Jesus Christ our Lord, to whom, with thee and the Holy Ghost, be all honour and glory, world without end. Amen.

I like to think that that her heart would lift, as the words were read, with a sense of thanksgiving. Thanksgiving, or the Greek word, Eucharist: it reminds us that what lies at the heart of Christianity is a sense of taking with thanks, rather than taking for granted. The art of gratitude: a habit of the heart which transforms resentment or pride or greed. She would hear the prayer giving thanks that God promises – vouchsafes – to feed us with the sacrament of Holy Communion, the Body and Blood of Christ. This God is in a real relationship with real people, subject to subject. The food is real sustenance, ingested so that those who receive become 'members incorporate in the mystical body of Jesus Christ'.

The prayer meditates on the gift of rich spiritual food that takes the human person to the heart of the mystery of God's love. That love is revealed as God became human in Jesus Christ, entering into the suffering and sacrifice that real love entails. Jesus Christ left behind the gift of a meal: bread and wine that is good and wholesome, signifying God's grace and benevolence. In eating and drinking these things, the human person becomes part of the mystical body which is 'the blessed company of all faithful people'. This is a company of those who eat bread together, transcending time and space. It is the ground and being of corporate life: the sacrament of the Body and Blood of Christ is what enables all human belonging to hold together. That belonging is ultimately realised when the Kingdom of God becomes reality, now to be hoped for. Such belonging and hoping cannot be achieved by human effort alone, but only by the merit gained for humanity by Jesus Christ who willingly entered into suffering and death to show God's love.

The prayer, Isabel might think, states an enormous amount for the Christian Church. To say that the sacrament of Holy Communion is where the grace of God explicitly enables corporate life and therefore true individuality is a massive claim: no less than that we are able to be properly corporate and properly individual because of God's love and grace at the heart of this and every Eucharist. Without God's grace, our human belonging becomes tenuous and strained, brittle, manifested in tribal and subhuman grouping. From this sacrament, then, all other corporate association draws its lifeblood.

The prayer also asks for grace to 'do all such good works as thou has prepared for us to walk in'. A lovely request, Isabel might think: that good works are actions that we walk in, confirming her in her desire to practise moral proximity, reaching out to those in need. The language of the prayer inspires the imagination, perhaps of the image of the Good Samaritan, walking along the road, and coming across his neighbour, and responding in love to the need before him.

# *Postscript*

This book began in a cafe at the University of Bradford. Professor Shaun Gregory and I were meeting for the first time to discuss my doing an MPhil. with him as supervisor at the Peace Studies Department in Bradford. We covered a lot of ground at some pace as we drank our coffees. Shaun quizzed me about the Anglican Church, concerned with how preoccupied it seemed with internal matters and issues of sexuality and gender, instead of engaging with cultural relativism and secularism. I remember his saying, in some exasperation, 'So what's the Church doing about it then?' I wasn't sure what he meant at the time, but over the months ahead the discussions continued. He introduced me to a different and unfamiliar literature, and this book is the result. I think it should prove topical, within an interesting contemporary national debate about the nature of society and where religion belongs in today's Western culture. I write as a priest in the Church of England, for those who are curious about Christianity and secularism, and who catch themselves wondering if the current debate is too shallow; whether there is more to it than this. I hope to convince that there is.

The Cathedral at Bradford allowed me study time for which I'm grateful. I miss friends and colleagues there, made during an exciting and happy time of ministry.

I have been privileged to have been granted some leave to write, leaving a busy St Edmundsbury Cathedral in the hands of talented and dedicated colleagues, both ordained and lay. I thank them all for their generosity and goodwill. My thanks to Peter and Hugh for their patience and Judy and Hubert for their support. Neighbours were kind as I wrote at Prospect Hill, particularly Karin and Alec Jones, Jim and Anne Baker, and Ruth Sutton. The time to think, read and write has been very special indeed, particularly at Ferrar House, Little Gidding, and thanks to Wendy and Paul Skirrow for their hospitality.

A number of other conversation partners have contributed to these pages, besides Shaun, or have offered comments and thoughts on the text. Vivienne Adshead, Nuzhat Ali, Geoff Barton, Ronald Blythe, Christopher Burdon, Liz Carnelley, Elizabeth Cook, Paul Daltry, Susan Durber, David Ison, Hilary Ison, David Jenkins, Wendy Kirk, Graeme Knowles, Robert Lawrance, Nigel McCulloch, Sara Maitland, Jessica Martin, Theo Poward, Peter Powell, Anna Rowlands, David Ruffley, Nigel Stock, Wahida Shaffi, Cherry Vann, Matthew Vernon, Thomas Ward and Vanessa Ward. I am grateful to each. Perhaps the greatest debt I owe is to the Littlemore Group, founded in 2005 in response to Archbishop Rowan Williams' call to the Anglican Church to recapture the imagination of the nation.

Caroline Chartres and Nicola Rusk at Bloomsbury have been unfailingly supportive through the process of generating the book. I have enjoyed working with them.

Frances Ward
Prospect Hill and Little Gidding
Ascension Day 2012

# Index of Names

Aquinas, St Thomas 137
Arendt, Hannah 13
Aristotle 78, 188
Avis, Paul 116

Bauman, Zygmunt 55ff
St Benedict 116n. 7, 219–25, 227–9,
    231, 233, 237
Bentham, Jeremy 75, 142ff, 146, 147,
    177, 183, 236
Blair, Tony 14, 18, 73, 75
Blake, William 207
Blond, Phillip 7n. 8, 17n. 1, 27n. 16,
    53, 59, 60, 206, 207
Botton, Alain de 26–7
Brown, Gordon 14, 18, 43n. 11, 73, 75
Burke, Edmund 77–81, 85, 88,
    93–106, 108, 110, 114, 117–21,
    125, 183, 200, 205, 206, 214,
    215, 236

Cameron, David 30n. 24, 33, 78
Carey, Peter 126, 127, 130, 131, 137,
    177
Cavanaugh, William T. 111, 113, 114
Crosland, Anthony 216

Dalhousie, Isabel see McCall Smith,
    Alexander

Dawkins, Richard 24n. 10, 26
Descartes, Rene 24
Donne, John 5, 13, 105–6, 153, 174

Eliot, T. S. 153

Field, Frank 43
Foucault, Michel 189–92, 191n. 29

Gale, Patrick 29, 149, 171, 197n. 2
Guardini, Romano 151–3, 156–7,
    177

Harris, Jose 72, 73
Hart, David Bentley 22n. 6, 23n. 7,
    29, 42, 112, 114, 188, 237
Hayek, Friedrich 72
Hegel, G. W. F. 186, 187n. 24, 190,
    193, 236
Herbert, George 138
Hitchens, Christopher 24n. 10
Hitchens, Peter 5n. 5, 149, 150, 162
Hobbes, Thomas 21, 22, 61, 64, 65, 69,
    70, 77–80, 82, 113, 114, 213
Hooker, Richard 80, 105, 106, 117,
    120
Hughes, John 137, 187n. 25

Judt, Tony 28n. 19, 72, 76–9

Lammy, David 11, 27n. 16, 33n. 2, 37,
    39n. 6, 41–4, 51, 54, 57, 70ff,
    208, 222–3
Larkin, Philip 193
Layard, Richard 13n. 15, 146
Locke, John 21, 65, 69, 78, 80, 113,
    114, 213

Malone, Gareth 211
Marr, Andrew 56, 74n. 13, 215–17
Marx, Karl 102, 187
McCabe, Herbert 152
McCall Smith, Alexander (passages
    from the Isabel Dalhousie
    books) 4, 7, 8–10, 20–1, 22–4,
    25, 31, 50–1, 56, 58, 61–3, 90,
    100–1, 132–3, 142, 150–1,
    155–6, 160, 163, 165–6,
    184–5, 189, 194, 198–9, 210,
    238
Mill, J. S. 75, 143–5, 147
Moreton, Cole 161
Morris, William 145

Nicholas of Cusa 116, 119n. 12
Nietzsche, Friedrich 21, 187–9
Norman, Jesse 75, 78–9, 98, 101n. 8,
    146, 206, 231, 232

Piaget, Jean 217
Putnam, Robert 206

Rawls, John 111
Rousseau, Jean-Jacques 1, 2, 21, 65,
    69–72, 73, 78, 79, 80–91, 93,
    99, 100, 113, 114, 120, 125,
    142, 193, 213, 215, 217, 236
Ruskin, John 145

Sacks, Jonathan 213–14
Said, Edward 192
Sartre, Jean Paul 188
Sayers, Dorothy L. 138n. 14
Scruton, Roger 5n. 4, 23n. 7, 24n. 10,
    26, 60–1, 65n. 18, 69n. 1, 81n.
    27, 133–6, 137n. 12, 147, 148,
    177, 178, 192n. 30
St Paul 6, 12, 13, 19, 80, 106–10, 114,
    115, 118, 120, 125, 129, 132,
    141, 172, 174, 175n. 16, 196,
    198, 224, 228, 237
St Thomas a Kempis 3, 197n. 2

Taylor, Charles 6, 19n. 3
Thatcher, Margaret 14, 18, 72–3, 75,
    81, 216

Williams, Rowan 41–2, 170n. 12,
    203–4, 213n. 16, 242
Winnicott, Donald 7, 152–3
Woodhead, Chris 218, 228n. 24
Wordsworth, William 143
Wright, Tom 195–6

# Index

aesthetic 61, 64, 126, 154, 184, 225, 235

agnosticism 21, 100, 119, 120, 237

American Revolution 95

Anglican Church 27–9, 117–19, 131ff, 148ff, 157, 159ff, 162–77, 178, 189–91, 226ff, 238ff

Anglican choral tradition 222–5

Anglican church schools 226ff

association, civil, voluntary 78, 81, 108, 116, 121, 125, 205–9, 211–14, 233, 236, 237, 240

art 1, 11, 26, 61, 64, 65, 70, 82, 89, 135ff, 153, 154, 156, 168, 225

atheism 2, 23n. 7, 26, 85, 99–100, 120

beauty 11, 24, 26, 126, 130, 131, 136, 144, 147, 152, 153, 156, 157, 225

benevolence 73, 76, 86, 239

Big Society 18, 75, 78, 121, 206, 214

Book of Common Prayer 135, 136, 151, 165, 238

broken Britain 7n. 8, 33

by heart 89, 105, 136, 172, 220, 225, 231

cathedrals 17, 35, 105, 118, 128, 205, 220, 222–5, 231–3, 241

character 4, 10, 11, 13, 14, 42, 44, 46, 57, 58, 61, 64, 66, 93, 132, 133, 146, 160, 161, 194, 195ff, 200–3, 204, 205, 209, 211, 212, 221, 225, 229, 230, 233–4, 237

child 6–7, 42, 93, 45, 52, 59, 71, 89, 152–3, 198, 202, 203ff, 213, 216, 222, 224–5, 227–9, 230–1

child-centredness 45, 89–90, 216–19, 222, 229

choirs 44, 205, 211, 222–5, 229, 231, 233

Church of England see Anglican Church

church-going 154–5, 160, 162, 190, 224, 237, 238

civil society 14, 64, 69, 78, 81, 82, 111, 121, 199, 205–14, 233

collective 5, 11, 12, 72, 83, 107–8, 110, 120

conciliarism, conciliar movement 115–20, 207

consumerism 55, 56, 74–5, 81, 145, 146, 203

corporate 3, 5ff, 10, 11, 12–13, 63, 66, 78, 80, 106, 108–9, 114–16, 120, 125, 157, 160, 169, 172, 176, 177, 183, 189, 190–1, 205, 207, 208, 211, 214, 219, 220, 225, 233, 237, 238–40

courtesy 198–9, 203, 206
cultural impoverishment 7, 42ff, 215, 227

death 25, 64, 65, 105, 147–8, 166, 168, 173–4, 178, 236, 240
delight 138, 147, 153, 155
democracy 56, 69, 86–8, 91, 96, 98–101, 115, 117, 120, 125, 236, 237

education 6, 7, 8, 14, 41, 42, 44–6, 64, 89–90, 103, 143, 205, 215–33
Education Act (1944) 226
emotion 13, 14, 41, 42, 43n. 10, 44, 45, 61, 64, 89, 135, 136, 147, 148, 151, 153, 160, 163, 168, 178, 215, 218, 225, 231, 232, 236, 237
empiricism 60, 144
Enlightenment 1, 2, 3, 14, 19, 22, 24n. 10, 49, 50, 61–2, 69, 85, 86, 100, 110–34, 142, 157, 183, 235
equality 2, 50, 55–6, 61, 65, 86, 172, 189
establishment, of the Church of England 27–8, 38, 117, 119, 226
Eucharist 12, 162, 175–9, 191, 238, 239, 240
evil 5, 50, 51, 60, 63, 64, 65, 101, 125, 132, 150, 185, 187, 188

failure 42, 44, 57, 109, 132ff, 138, 139, 148, 149
family 17n. 1, 41, 58, 59, 60, 71, 74, 89, 103, 200–2, 206, 212, 213, 214
fascism 5, 60, 73
fear 5, 17n. 1, 52, 57, 106, 109, 147–52, 155–6, 174, 193, 212, 237

feminism 57, 193
forgiveness 131, 132, 141, 150, 155, 163, 164, 165, 168, 193, 194, 204, 224, 229
freedom 2, 6, 55, 69, 70–4, 79, 80–2, 84, 86, 88, 98–9, 102–4, 106, 107, 112, 134, 154, 174, 187, 193, 203, 206, 217
French Revolution 85, 88, 95, 100, 104, 125
friendship 6, 23, 209, 214

gang culture 11ff, 37, 39, 101, 108, 184
general will (Rousseau's concept of) 84ff, 87, 88
gift 45, 135–6, 142, 147, 148, 167, 173ff, 177, 233, 239
Golden Rule 2, 229
Good Samaritan 185, 187n. 24, 205, 240
governance 27, 99, 101n. 8, 116n. 7, 118, 190, 206, 208, 226
gratitude 135ff, 148, 160, 233, 238ff
greatest good for the greatest number 143, 145, 147, 196
greed 13, 18, 39, 40, 46, 51, 72, 109, 133, 150, 164, 173, 212, 239
grievance 40, 42, 44, 54, 55, 184, 185, 192, 194, 233

happiness 2, 4, 13, 14, 41, 134, 143, 145ff, 183, 189, 196, 215, 232
hedonism 42, 146–7, 156, 231
Holy Communion *see* Eucharist
homo economicus 74ff, 227–8
House of Commons 97, 98, 101, 118
House of Lords 97, 98, 101, 118, 119, 237
human dignity 43n. 10, 141, 144, 215, 232

human nature 50, 65, 69, 70, 75, 79, 125, 144, 145, 160, 176, 200, 205, 216, 218, 220, 235

identity 3, 8–9, 11, 12, 14, 35, 37, 54, 58, 103, 106, 108, 110, 161, 164, 165, 172, 183–94, 197, 199, 204, 211, 213, 219, 233ff
identity politics 58, 183–94
ideology 19, 22n. 6, 50, 59, 61, 75, 80, 89–90, 193, 217, 222, 229
imagination 7, 14, 19, 20, 29, 30, 42, 45, 65, 86, 130, 137, 141, 143, 147, 155, 164, 178, 211, 240
individualism 3, 5, 8, 45, 53, 72, 90, 104, 125, 183, 233, 235, 236
individuality 10–12, 77, 105, 106, 108, 125, 169, 172, 219, 224, 228, 233, 235, 240
inequality 17n. 1, 56, 73n. 22
innovation 22–3, 102, 143
institution 22, 24, 39, 44n. 12, 52, 53, 59–61, 76–9, 81, 96, 98–9, 102, 112, 115–17, 121, 125, 153, 177, 183, 189, 190, 207
instrumentality 3, 6, 44, 66, 126, 131, 137, 138, 142, 144, 148, 152, 161, 177, 203, 211, 214, 228, 233, 235, 236
Islam 34, 35n. 8, 192, 201–3

Joseph Rowntree Foundation 5, 36, 55
joy 17n. 1, 41, 64, 135–6, 138, 141, 146, 152, 155, 167, 173, 177, 178, 228, 233
judgement 46, 51, 53, 95, 150, 155, 156, 188

law 34, 38–9, 41, 57, 65, 69, 80, 82, 83, 85, 86, 88, 97, 98, 101n. 8, 108, 114, 115, 120, 141, 143

law giver, the (Rousseau's concept of) 85
liberal egalitarianism 2, 49–63, 71–3, 111–14, 119, 133, 222
little platoons (Burke's concept of) 77, 78, 79, 108, 121, 205, 206–7, 214, 236
loss 131, 132–4, 136, 147, 177, 189, 236
loss of faith 61, 65, 127, 130
love 10, 25, 29–30, 41, 62–6, 134–6, 138, 141, 144, 152n. 25, 168, 171, 173–4, 176, 196–8, 202, 219, 228
love of neighbour 55, 64–6, 150, 155, 157, 160, 166, 179, 183, 204, 221, 229–30, 233, 236–40

market 7n. 8, 44, 56, 71, 73–4, 81, 146, 183, 203, 206, 207, 215
marriage 59
marriage, arranged 201–2
master and slave 186–93
materialism 7, 42, 55, 62, 65, 76, 81, 145, 156, 203–4, 215
meritocracy 101, 120
monarchy 83, 96–101, 117–19, 125, 236
monetarism *see* neo-liberalism
money 37, 40, 43, 73, 208
moral proximity 170, 240
moral vacuum 42, 46, 50, 51, 202–4, 227
morality 4, 13, 14, 21, 24, 25, 44–5, 49, 50–4, 66, 69n. 1, 76, 79, 80, 94, 135–6, 142, 147, 150, 153, 157, 160, 163, 178, 183, 187–200, 202, 204–5, 214, 215, 225, 230, 231–8
music 1, 11, 23, 56, 57, 61, 135, 136, 154, 159, 160, 222–5, 231–2

narcissism 44, 56, 64, 74, 89, 90, 91,
    155, 164, 183, 215, 219, 231,
    232, 233
neo-liberalism 14, 18, 72, 81
nihilism 42, 57, 64, 188
nudge 230

parenting 41, 43n. 11, 71–2, 74, 89,
    193–4, 201–4, 209, 217
philanthropy 19, 94, 212–13
play 6–7, 10, 138–9, 151–3, 157,
    159–60, 178, 203, 213, 237
Plowden Report, the 217–18
police 35, 36, 37, 38, 39, 41, 42, 43, 46,
    53, 71, 209
political thought 6, 21–2, 63, 65,
    75–9, 80, 82, 95, 100–1, 106,
    110–21, 177, 183, 207, 213,
    235, 236
post-colonialism 192
poverty 17n. 1, 18, 37, 43, 46, 65, 73n.
    11, 79, 109, 212, 227
power 39, 69, 82, 83, 87, 88, 96–101,
    109, 115–20, 166–7, 187–8,
    189–91, 192, 193–4, 207, 214,
    235, 236–7
practice, -ality 3, 11, 19, 28, 30, 41,
    53, 89, 126, 130, 131, 137, 154,
    156, 175, 177–9, 190, 198, 203,
    208, 219, 222, 228, 231, 232n.
    26, 237–8
prayer 128, 136, 137, 152, 154, 161,
    163, 167, 170–2, 175, 209, 220,
    238–40
public service 18, 29, 46, 55, 64, 93,
    97, 99, 100, 183, 205, 229, 231

racism 17n. 1, 37
rationalism 2, 6, 22n. 6, 24, 26, 102,
    126, 137, 144, 148, 156, 157,
    178, 236

religion 5n. 5, 11, 23–30, 49, 62–3,
    76, 78n. 21, 79–80, 86–7, 100,
    111–19, 127, 132–6, 142, 144,
    147, 149, 155, 159, 177, 188,
    201, 204, 221, 226–8, 231, 233,
    235, 241
repudiation 57–61, 65, 209–10, 214
resentment 18, 36, 37, 39, 41, 44,
    54–8, 91, 164–5, 184, 188,
    192–4, 233, 234, 239
responsibility 13n. 14, 18, 19, 43, 52,
    54, 55, 57, 70, 71, 73n. 9, 80,
    81, 103, 109, 151, 164, 165,
    187, 203, 224, 233
rights 5, 9, 49–50, 53–8, 74, 76, 78,
    83–4, 86, 88, 94, 109, 135, 164,
    173, 177
riots 14, 18, 33, 35–47, 57, 70–1, 75,
    80, 87
Roman Catholic Church 27, 59, 115,
    118, 151, 221, 222, 226
romanticism 1, 70, 74, 80, 87, 88–91,
    125, 142, 203, 217

safeguarding 52n. 3
secular 1–3, 6, 14, 19, 22n. 6, 24, 30,
    46–7, 49, 64, 65–6, 70, 64,
    80, 81, 86, 91, 100, 104, 106,
    111–20, 135, 137, 139, 141–9,
    156, 160, 167, 177, 178, 183,
    186, 193, 218, 226, 233, 235–7,
    241
self-interest 13, 18, 62, 64, 66, 70, 75,
    81, 93, 142, 144, 150, 160, 200,
    213, 228, 237
self sacrifice 64, 160, 174, 188, 225,
    228, 237
shame 9, 39, 43, 149, 151, 164, 165,
    190
social contract 21, 22, 69, 78–80, 82,
    86, 88, 115, 119, 183, 213

state 7n. 8, 22n. 6, 43n. 10, 51, 53,
    72–3, 75, 76, 78, 81–6, 97, 102,
    111–18, 183, 206, 207, 214, 222

time 3, 22, 103, 135, 151–3, 155,
    167–9, 174, 178, 202, 204, 206,
    220, 225, 237, 239
toleration, tolerance 2, 49, 50–3, 66,
    71, 86, 112
tradition 1, 3, 9, 19, 22–4, 27, 30, 53,
    59, 63, 69, 70, 77–8, 81, 89, 99,
    102–4, 115, 119, 131, 135–6,
    153, 157, 162, 175n. 16, 206,
    208, 217, 222–5, 229, 231, 236
trust 13, 17n. 1, 50–3, 60, 78, 95, 103,
    104, 109, 160, 163, 200, 204,
    211, 213

us and them 33n. 2, 184, 185–93
utilitarianism 3, 6, 7n. 8, 11, 13, 44,
    46, 66, 75, 104, 126, 142–7,
    156, 161, 177–8, 183, 186,
    196, 211, 224, 228, 233, 235,
    236
utopianism 1, 22, 23, 102, 104, 132,
    133, 136, 218

victim 54, 57, 151, 164, 185, 191, 193,
    193n. 31, 194
virtue 13, 43, 53, 58, 60, 64, 78, 82,
    95, 109, 112, 131, 132, 141,
    142, 146, 196, 199, 200, 203–5,
    211, 220, 224, 228–9, 230, 231,
    234, 237
volunteering 52, 179, 205–14

work 17n. 1, 41, 73–4, 137–9, 141–2,
    146, 147–8, 186, 187n. 25, 223,
    224, 231
worship 12, 19, 27, 138, 148–79, 183,
    190, 191, 204, 222ff, 234, 237,
    238